# WIDE PUBLISHING FOR AUTHORS

A GUIDE TO EXPANDING YOUR BOOK'S REACH AND FINDING MORE READERS

# DALE L. ROBERTS

Wide Publishing for Authors: A Guide to Expanding Your Book's Reach and Finding More Readers

All rights reserved.

Copyright ©2024 One Jacked Monkey, LLC

- eBook ISBN: 978-1-63925-059-2
- Paperback ISBN: 978-1-63925-060-8
- Hardcover ISBN: 978-1-63925-061-5
- Audiobook ISBN: 978-1-63925-062-2

No part of this book may be reproduced in any form by any electronic or mechanical means, including information storage and retrieval systems, without permission in writing from the copyright owner, except by a reviewer who may quote brief passages in a review.

Some recommended links in this book are part of affiliate programs. If you purchase a product through one of the links, then I get a portion of each sale. It doesn't affect your cost and greatly helps support the cause. If you have any reservations about buying a product through my affiliate link, then Google a direct link and bypass the affiliate link.

# TABLE OF CONTENTS

PREFACE: UNDERSTANDING THE PUBLISHING MODELS ........................ 1

INTRODUCTION ........................................................ 4

CHAPTER 1: EXCLUSIVE DISTRIBUTION VS. WIDE DISTRIBUTION: WHY WIDE? ... 8

CHAPTER 2: AMAZON ALTERNATIVES ..................................... 16

    AMAZON ALTERNATIVE #1: APPLE BOOKS FOR AUTHORS ............. 18

    AMAZON ALTERNATIVE #2 BARNES & NOBLE PRESS ................ 22

    AMAZON ALTERNATIVE #3: KOBO WRITING LIFE .................. 26

    AMAZON ALTERNATIVE #4: GOOGLE PLAY BOOKS PARTNER CENTER .... 32

CHAPTER 3: AGGREGATE PUBLISHING ..................................... 36

    AGGREGATE PUBLISHER #1: DRAFT2DIGITAL ........................ 41

    AGGREGATE PUBLISHER #2: INGRAMSPARK ......................... 45

    AGGREGATE PUBLISHER #3: BOOKVAULT .......................... 55

    AGGREGATE PUBLISHER #4: PUBLISHDRIVE ........................ 59

    AGGREGATE PUBLISHER #5: LULU ................................ 66

AGGREGATE PUBLISHER FOR AUDIOBOOKS #1:
FINDAWAY VOICES BY SPOTIFY ........................................ 73

AGGREGATE PUBLISHER FOR AUDIOBOOKS #2: AUTHOR'S REPUBLIC .... 77

CHAPTER 4: MISCELLANEOUS AGGREGATE PUBLISHERS ..................... 83

CHAPTER 5: SELF-DISTRIBUTION/DIRECT SALES ......................... 90

CHAPTER 6: WHERE TO START ......................................... 96

CHAPTER 7: WIDE PUBLISHING FOR EBOOKS ............................ 100

THE WIDE PUBLISHING CHECKLIST FOR EBOOKS ..................... 106

CHAPTER 8: WIDE PUBLISHING FOR PRINT BOOKS ...................... 109

THE WIDE PUBLISHING CHECKLIST FOR PRINT BOOKS ................ 115

CHAPTER 9: WIDE PUBLISHING FOR AUDIOBOOKS ....................... 118

THE WIDE PUBLISHING CHECKLIST FOR AUDIOBOOKS ................ 122

CHAPTER 10: DO YOUR RESEARCH ..................................... 125

CONCLUSION ....................................................... 136

BEFORE YOU GO... ................................................. 138

ABOUT THE AUTHOR ................................................. 139

SPECIAL THANKS ................................................... 141

RESOURCES ........................................................ 143

REFERENCES ....................................................... 144

🚀 **Launch Your Book to #1 Bestseller Status on Amazon—For FREE!**
Are you ready to make your book a hit on Amazon? Download my **Proven Bestseller Book Launch Checklist**—absolutely FREE!

This isn't just any checklist. It's the same system I've used to launch **dozens of books** to #1 bestseller status in over a dozen regions on Amazon—even in some of the most **hyper-competitive categories.** Whether you're gearing up for a launch or firing off a preorder campaign, this **step-by-step plan** will help you rank fast.

💡 **Here's the kicker:** This exclusive checklist is ONLY available when you subscribe to my email newsletter—your **insider guide** to the latest self-publishing news, tips, and strategies.

🗓 Once to twice a week, I'll deliver:

- **Exclusive industry secrets** to get ahead of the curve
- **Proven marketing tactics** that actually work
- Advance updates on changes in the world of self-publishing

Join thousands of authors who have already used this checklist to **boost their book's visibility** and take their self-publishing career to the next level.

🔥 Don't wait—this checklist is **only available for a limited time.**

✉ Subscribe now and grab your free checklist at: **DaleLinks.com/Checklist.**

# DRAFT 2 DIGITAL®

## Next level tools to help you grow.

Whether you're an aspiring author or international bestseller, we've got the tools to help you publish faster, distribute wider and manage your business easier.

Learn more by going to **d2d.tips/dale** and read on to discover some of what sets D2D apart:

- ✓ Automated end-matter
- ✓ New Release Notifications for readers
- ✓ Payment Splitting for contributors
- ✓ Scheduled price changes
- ✓ Smashwords store coupons
- ✓ Universal Book Links via Books2Read.com

### It's print-on-demand reimagined.

Create a paperback on draft2digital.com from your existing ebook with just a few clicks, and **create a full, wrap-around book cover from your ebook cover**. It really is that easy!

### THE indie bookstore.

Massive annual sales, self-serve promotion tools, and the **industry's best royalty rates** of up to 80% list. Readers love discovering breakout indie authors at smashwords.com.

# Win **awards** and get **reviews** for **your book**

25% off your first purchase

bookawardpro.com

"I've used dozens of book cover design services over the last ten years, and none compare to the level of quality and professionalism that Miblart delivers."

— **Dale L. Roberts**

## Miblart - a book cover design company for self-published authors

| Designers who specialize in different genres | Unlimited number of revisions |
|---|---|
| No deposit to get started | You can pay in installments |

**GET A BOOK COVER THAT WILL BECOME YOUR Nº1 MARKETING TOOL**

Excellent

 4.9

# Get Your Book Publish-Ready with Dibbly

Meet **Dibbly Create**.  Your All-in-1 A.I. companion for writing, publishing & marketing your book.

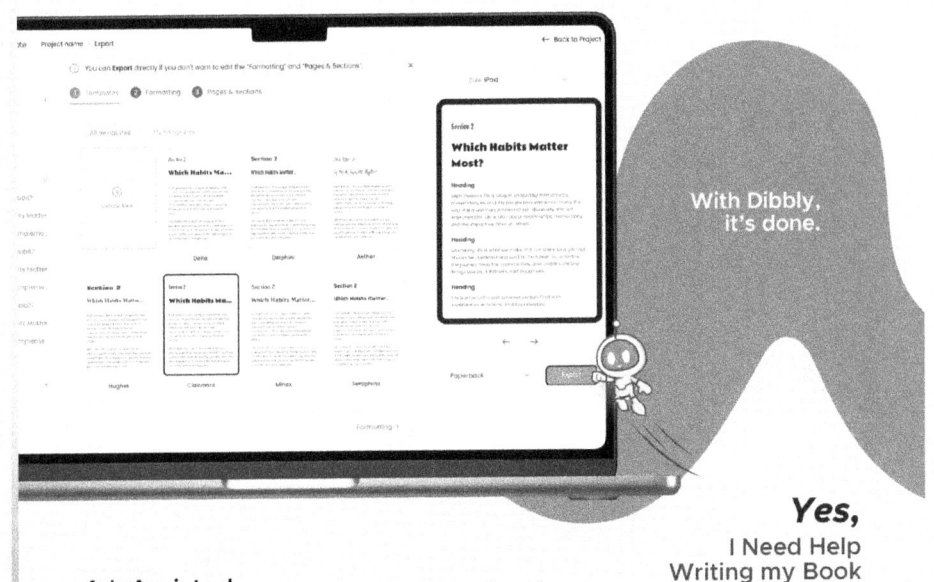

With Dibbly, it's done.

**Yes,**
I Need Help Writing my Book

## A.I. Assisted:

- ✓ Deep Formatting Controls
- ✓ Powerful Formatting Tools
- ✓ Highly-Customizable Book Layout
- ✓ Exporting Templates
- ✓ Device Preview (Multiple Devices)
- ✓ Export in EPUB
- ✓ Much More

## Try for Free!

Scan the QR Code or visit

# PREFACE:
# UNDERSTANDING THE PUBLISHING MODELS

The publishing industry has a ton of insider lingo that might not make sense to you or which you have yet to explore. Understanding the publishing models will help you maneuver around potential pitfalls and brick walls. It's easy to get overwhelmed or misinformed, especially if you aren't familiar with this business.

**Traditional publishing** is the process in which you submit your manuscript to established publishing houses. If your work is accepted for publication and put under contract, the publisher will then handle editing, design, production, distribution, and marketing your book. You may receive an advance payment and your contract should outline royalties you'll be paid from book sales, but you relinquish some control over the publishing process. This pathway can be competitive and lengthy, requiring you to go through either literary agents or lengthy direct submissions to publishers. None of the recommendations in this book pertain to traditional publishing.

**Self-publishing** means you publish books without a traditional publisher. You take full responsibility for editing, designing, producing, and marketing your work. This approach allows for complete creative control and a higher share of the profits, but it also requires more time, effort, and personal resources.

**Hybrid publishing** combines elements of both traditional and self-publishing, giving you the opportunity to leverage the benefits of both approaches. This model creates a partnership that supports authors in reaching a wider audience while allowing them to maintain some creative control.

**Vanity publishing** involves you paying a publisher to have your work published. This model rarely involves quality checkpoints—there is often little to no selection process, so if you pay the publisher, they will publish your book whether it's marketable or not. Under this model, you typically pay costs for printing, distribution, and marketing, and the publisher may not provide high quality editing and covers, although they may include some support and services. This pathway can lead to low-quality publications, since the focus for the publisher is on generating revenue from authors, not selling your books to readers.

Hybrid publishing and vanity publishing seem similar on the surface, so you can easily confuse them if you're not careful. With hybrid publishing, you pay for specific services while retaining control over your work. Conversely, vanity publishing requires you to pay a substantial upfront fee but as I mentioned, you cannot assume quality editing and covers will be provided for the price you pay, which can lead to potentially low-value product.

When considering these options, carefully review contracts for clarity around rights and royalties. Always investigate a company's reputation and track record in the publishing industry. Word of mouth goes a long way, so ask around in a community of authors and peers. I've found indie authors are a loyal bunch who'll warn most new authors of the dangers in vanity publishing. Always look for full transparency in costs to avoid hidden fees. Vanity publishing companies often withhold information about additional fees until you require a specific service, at which point they may strongly encourage you to invest in an expensive upgrade that might not provide the best value.

The ALLi Watchdog List and the Writer Beware website are two excellent resources for identifying and dealing with problematic individuals or entities in the publishing world. I include all references and resources mentioned throughout this book in the back.

In this book, I focus exclusively on the self-publishing model, and specifically self-publishing wide. If you want complete creative control over your work, full transparency around costs, and the possibility of reaching readers anywhere they are, self-publishing wide may be the right choice for you.

# INTRODUCTION

My indie heavy metal band finally made it! As a small-time music group, we performed in shady dive bars to packed clubs. By the late '90s, we were finally gaining traction and performing anywhere and everywhere. In every venue we played, we sold crude self-made merch and DIY cassette tapes of our music. Did we make millions? Not by any stretch, but we were young, hungry, and ready to do whatever it took to get our music in front of more listeners.

Considered by our peers to be talentless and entirely too arrogant for our own good, we survived and even thrived in the pre-internet era of music. This happened before the emergence of Napster and many other online music services. Somehow, though, we found a way to remain in people's minds and make a laughable part-time income. We were all young and had day jobs to support our budding music careers, but we knew it was a matter of time before the music industry would eat up all our time and resources as we searched for success. The problem was we didn't have a clue about how to reach more people.

When I picked up the popular heavy metal magazine *Circus*, I saw a featured post about up-and-coming metal acts that gave me a tremendous idea. Getting placement in *Circus* was free; all we had

## INTRODUCTION

to do was submit a brief bio, a band picture, and a short demo tape. I forked up the money to ship all that out and hoped for the best. A few months later, I made a monumental discovery while browsing the selection at the magazine rack.

Toward the back of the latest edition, my band had landed a fairly prominent spot for up-and-coming acts. I was beyond excited and bought every magazine on the rack, then went to other stores and did the same thing until I had a big stack to hand out to anyone willing to receive a copy. Mind you, this was a big deal. Back then, you could not Tweet about anything or share content on social media. Heck, I don't even think MySpace was a sparkle in Tom Anderson's eyes at that time.

Since the featured spot included a way to contact us, a ton of mail flooded in. In fact, after that, we received the first ever "fan mail" of our lengthy yet tumultuous career. One letter after the other requested more details about our music, where we were playing, and how to stay in touch. Heck, we created our very own snail mail newsletter. That used to cost us more to manage than we made, but we were geeked up to reach a wider audience than we had before.

We had unknowingly submitted to a magazine with global distribution, so heavy metal fans from every corner of the United States and even as far as Israel got to know us. As a result, we found one of our most dedicated and loyal fans in Suri, a young girl living in Israel. She became our #1 fan, someone we'd send postcards to on a near weekly basis. Months into our pen pal arrangement with Suri, she let us know with a heavy heart that we wouldn't hear from her for a while because she was slated to join the Israeli military. Even though she could hardly afford to pay for our music or merchandise, we always found a way to accommodate her.

How crazy is it that an American metal band could connect with a fan in Israel well before email became as widely used as it is now? We knew we had a good thing going, and we were thankful every day for the likes of Suri and scores of other fans. Just imagine if we hadn't submitted to this magazine: Where would we be? Would we have the same treasured memories of being in a dysfunctional rock group? I believe this opportunity breathed life into our band and ignited our ambition to new levels. Did we capitalize on it? Possibly not enough, but that's another story for another day.

The magic of reaching every corner of the world without investing in more than a little postage was pretty amazing back then. The good news is, if you're an author you can reach far wider than our band could have ever dreamed of back in the mid- to late '90s. Even though we were producing music and you're publishing books, you'll be able to draw some parallels between my backstory and the topic of this book—publishing wide.

Publishing wide means that you distribute your books to every imaginable platform in an attempt to reach more readers. Sometimes, this equates to more revenue. Practically, it means making your books more accessible by not limiting yourself to only the most popular retail sites.

The good news for you is that you won't have to mail out your manuscript like we mailed our cassette to a magazine. Heck, you may never have to send a single copy of your book to a reader. When you publish your book wide, the retail sites that sell your book handle shipping for you. Meanwhile, you can write your next manuscript or promote any backlog of books you may have.

The more concerning news is that you're going to have to put in some work to make publishing wide possible. Successfully publishing on multiple platforms is not as simple as writing the book and then pushing a button. Uploading to any random site in any order won't do, because you might miss opportunities for better reach and decent payout.

After publishing hundreds of books online across scores of platforms, I have the experience and insights you need to march forward confidently and publish your books to the widest audience. Sure, you could Google your way through the best steps for publishing wide, but that's fraught with dangers, peril, and all kinds of headaches if you aren't careful.

*Wide Publishing for Authors* includes the practical steps to get your book onto as many virtual and physical retail shelves as possible. I break down all the steps you need to understand what you should do and why. It's not enough for you to agree with my recommendations. You need to comprehend why each site might be good for you and if that path actually fits into your goals as an author.

If you don't have the patience to hear me out on each avenue and its merits, skip ahead to the guide for the type of publication you're selling:

- Ebooks
- Print books
- Audiobooks

Before you skip to those sections, I implore you to hear me out. Not all avenues I recommend will resonate with you. Some suggestions will be unsuitable for a few authors. At the very least, you'll get insights into how I get my books onto more online retailers.

Assuming you're ready to get to work, let's dig in!

# CHAPTER 1:
# EXCLUSIVE DISTRIBUTION VS. WIDE DISTRIBUTION: WHY WIDE?

These days, you don't have to look far to find someone who knows a little about the self-publishing business. Most indie authors know how to publish on Amazon through Kindle Direct Publishing (KDP) and Audiobook Creation Exchange (ACX). While there's nothing inherently wrong with publishing through those avenues, it's rather short-sighted for some authors since Amazon doesn't reach every nook and cranny of the world.

Though Amazon dominates online retail today, it's not the only player in the market. In fact, scores of online retailers reach different audiences in other parts of the world. Whether a region doesn't get Amazon distribution or a customer is outright against supporting the online juggernaut, ignoring Amazon alternatives is like saying those customers aren't worthy of reading your content. Sure, you wouldn't actually say that, nor do you imply that. But the fact remains that if you exclude any options beyond Amazon, you may not view other platforms as viable. I'll argue that if you aren't willing to reach any/all customers, you're leaving out a lot of readers.

## CHAPTER 1: EXCLUSIVE DISTRIBUTION VS. WIDE DISTRIBUTION: WHY WIDE?

When you hear the term publish wide, that means publishing beyond just Amazon. Yes, publishing on Amazon may be the path of least resistance, but it's not the only path to reaching new readers.

## A BALANCED LOOK AT EXCLUSIVE DISTRIBUTION: AMAZON KDP & ACX

KDP and ACX are self-publishing distribution platforms owned by Amazon. With KDP, you can sell ebook, paperback, and hardcover books on many Amazon platforms and some partner sites. If you're publishing ebooks, KDP distributes your ebook to thirteen Amazon marketplaces. For print books, KDP distributes to twelve Amazon marketplaces (paperback) or nine (hardcover). ACX publishes your audiobook to Amazon, Audible, and Apple—which, if you're keeping count, is the smallest of the three, distributing to only three marketplaces.

Audible commands about 63.4% of today's online downloadable audiobook market.[i] However, that doesn't mean you're beholden to that platform alone. After all, you didn't write and produce a book simply to appear in just three marketplaces, right?

If you dive deep into the KDP platform, you may find some confusing information. No matter what program you take part in, Amazon does not require exclusivity for print books. You can still sell your print books widely, even if you distribute ebooks through KDP Select or audiobooks exclusively through ACX.

Conversely, KDP Select is an exclusive program that applies to ebooks. When authors enroll their ebooks in KDP Select, they agree to Amazon-only distribution of that title for ninety days. KDP Select distribution is renewable for additional consecutive periods after the first ninety days unless the book is unenrolled. This means that the author cannot distribute any electronic version of their book in any format anywhere except on Amazon.

Will they find out if you do? Well, you'd be amazed at how observant Amazon is. Never doubt their ability to find authors breaking the ninety-day agreement. Some authors inadvertently run afoul of the KDP Select agreement; and when they get caught, they will either receive a warning or a more serious penalty—account suspension.

To publish wide, you must deselect the KDP Select option to prevent the agreement from renewing. If you're already enrolled in KDP Select, you need to fulfill any remaining time in the agreement before going wide.

ACX is a bit more complicated. Should you want to publish your audiobook through ACX, you have two options: exclusive and non-exclusive. ACX rewards exclusive audiobooks with a higher royalty rate of 40%. For those who choose non-exclusive distribution, ACX pays a significantly lower royalty of 25%. Authors often ask me if it's worth going wide with an audiobook; my answer is always the same:

> *What is your goal as an author? Do you want to reach more readers? Or make more money?*

You will reach more readers publishing wide, but I cannot guarantee you'll make more money. Some authors earn more publishing their audiobook wide. Most authors break even at best with audiobooks. Based on your genre, your production quality, marketing, and many other factors, you won't know the best avenue for your audiobooks until you try several.

## CHAPTER 1: EXCLUSIVE DISTRIBUTION VS. WIDE DISTRIBUTION: WHY WIDE?

Like KDP Select, the ACX distribution agreement for each audiobook requires exclusivity for ninety days. An important exception to this is if you've produced an audiobook on a royalty split agreement. By avoiding upfront narrator costs via a royalty split, you'll be bound to your agreement's terms, potentially staying with ACX for at least seven years.

If you've paid to produce your audiobook and have no restrictions or contracts that require exclusivity for the narrators to get paid, you can start with exclusive ACX distribution. Like with KDP Select, you can unenroll after the initial enrollment period ends. To change your distribution agreement to non-exclusive, contact support@acx.com. Once you are not exclusively bound to ACX, you can publish your audiobook anywhere and everywhere, including some avenues few other self-publishing resources discuss. I'll cover those later.

Publishing exclusively to KDP and ACX has both pros and cons. Ultimately, it's up to you which is better for your business. However, this is a book about publishing wide, so I encourage you to consider how exclusive distribution with any Amazon platform might limit your book's reach. One example is library distribution. Libraries cannot purchase ebooks and audio books that are exclusive to KDP Select and ACX. That's why many successful and large authors don't have work on the library apps even if they have a paperback on the library shelf. The ebook and audiobooks may be bound to exclusive distribution agreements, which means even libraries cannot purchase those copies to be distributed to library patrons.

With a singular publishing method, you will have fewer dashboards and tax forms to manage at the end of the year. That may sound far easier when you're just starting out. After publishing wide since 2015, I'm well aware it takes more time to publish wide than it does having my content exclusively on Amazon. Thankfully, I have published wide enough times that it's second nature to me now—and that's why I want to share with you why I've chosen to distribute this way.

The biggest drawbacks of sticking with only Amazon platforms include a limited or potentially smaller audience reach and the major issue—the potential risk of losing it all as the result of the slightest misstep. While you might never try to step over an invisible line set by Amazon in their ambiguous guidelines, some authors have. In my book, *The Amazon Self Publisher*, I shared the true story of someone I know who earned more than $100,000 per month in ebook sales. He went all-in on KDP and didn't even bother building a website or an email list. That author did not even format his books into any other iterations beyond ebooks. Amazon terminated his account one day, told him he knew what he did, and then moved on. He lost his income, his audience, and his only distribution avenue.

The reality is…

> *You are only one mistake away from Amazon terminating your account.*

If you're not completely convinced this could happen to you, I recommend taking a moment to google it. Many forums, blog posts, and videos cover how authors have run afoul of Amazon; it's astounding. Let's be clear, you do not have to do anything intentional for Amazon to nix your account. It doesn't matter how big your following is or if all the evidence you have to share is in your favor. When Amazon upholds its decision to close an account, that's it. It's over. Do not pass go; do not collect $200. You go straight to publishing purgatory.

Rather than allowing that to happen, start by expanding your publications to more avenues. Let's analyze the pros and cons of wide publishing. While exclusive distribution is simpler and can offer higher royalty rates, I recommend all authors consider publishing wide. Although wide publishing requires more work, steps, and management, it allows you to avoid giving any one platform complete control over your business—including the risk of being shut down for accidental infractions. Let's now take a thorough look at publishing wide.

## A BALANCED LOOK AT WIDE DISTRIBUTION

If my introduction wasn't enough to sell you on wide distribution, then let's explore why it may or may not be a good fit for you. Yes, the purpose of publishing wide is to reach more readers. Publishing to KDP and ACX alone will give you access to a lot of online customers, but not *all* customers. Amazon isn't everywhere. Heck, aggregate publishing platform PublishDrive reaches China!

Yep, China. And, you do not have to translate your book to get access.

Scroll through your KDP and ACX dashboards and you won't see that country listed. Will Amazon distribute to China eventually? Maybe. But rather than wait for that day, why not just go there now?

The biggest drawback to publishing wide is the time involved in managing your accounts. Between the many dashboards, publishing or updating books, and the tax forms, you're going to invest quite a bit more administrative time. Yes, it's a lot to manage at first, but eventually, you'll get a system in place that'll help you navigate it all much faster. Just be patient.

## WHY I CHOSE TO SHOWCASE THESE PLATFORMS

Any time I share information, I speak from first-hand experience. Rather than tell you what you could otherwise find through a Google search, I want you to hear the human aspect of publishing.

I'm going to share what it's like publishing to several platforms. I'll explain whether I would recommend alternatives, and I'll explore what authors stand to benefit from each avenue.

I will also provide additional resources you can investigate beyond what I recommend in this book. I simply don't have enough time and money to pursue every option available for self-publishing online. There may be platforms I have heard of but not tried myself. In those cases, I'll share information, but please investigate any option you consider. Do your due diligence. And no matter what you think of a specific platform's features, at some point when you publish wide, ask this question:

> *Does publishing to this platform provide any additional revenue or readers?*

If yes, then go for it. If not, move on. If it's a maybe, then you'll have to try it out for yourself.

I apply the same philosophy to self-publishing as I do to advertising: Don't invest more than you can afford to lose. While some options may seem stellar—like a platform's excellent reach or high royalties—they often come with drawbacks, such as subscription fees or large upfront payments. Those options might work well for some authors, but many indie authors struggle to afford even basic expenses, like a professional cover design. In that case, spending $3,000 to publish through a single platform—even for wide publishing—isn't a good fit.

My selections are based on my experience grinding it out and saving every penny earned just so I can put food on the table. I never pay to distribute my book if I can help it. I'll share some exceptions to the rule shortly.

I want to focus on the four major Amazon alternatives, as well as aggregate publishing companies that will distribute your book for a slight cut of your net profits. Keep in mind, my experience is based on the genres I have published in and many other factors. Use this book as a tool—not a bible. You'll learn some of what's worked for me, but like every small business, only you can decide how to best run your author brand. What works for me might not work for you. By the end of this book, you will have a lot more information about the publishing wide experience—both positive and negative.

# CHAPTER 2:
# AMAZON ALTERNATIVES

In my award-winning publication *Secrets of the Permafree Book*, I revealed Amazon will not allow you to price your ebook as free. Why is that? Well, it makes sense as a business model. If they take a percentage of every sale, they make nothing when you sell a book for free. There is one workaround to this…

If Amazon discovers your ebook has a different price elsewhere, they are eager to know. Make no mistake, they don't care about small online businesses or local mom-and-pop bookstores. Amazon only cares when your ebook sells below their price on other major online distributors. They care because they will sell your book at the price it's available at some competing retailers. Not all, but some.

Who is the competition that Amazon deems enough of a threat as to price match even if that means selling your book for free? It's simple:

1. Apple Books
2. Barnes & Noble Press
3. Kobo
4. Google Play Books

When I first discovered how to price my book free, I didn't know about these alternatives and that publishing to these sites made a world of difference. No would-be self-publishing expert ever shared how I make my ebook free on Amazon. I had to learn this strategy through my former coach and mentor. Even though he knew how to do it, he didn't have a firm grasp on which platforms Amazon would price match. As a result, my first few attempts at price matching were rather frustrating.

That brings me to my topic for this chapter: alternatives to Amazon. Not all alternatives are created equally. Amazon views some platforms as competition, while others aren't significant enough to draw its attention.

For example, when I tried publishing my ebook through Smashwords, setting the price as free or $0.00, then asking Amazon to price match my ebook in the Smashwords store, guess what happened? Of course, Amazon refused. They gave me a boilerplate reply: "We retain the discretion to price match your book…" Yada yada… It was their way of saying, "No, and we won't tell you why."

I didn't learn until I published my third ebook wide as permafree that Amazon only considers real competitors for their price-matching policy. After publishing dozens of books wide, I'm fairly confident now Amazon only matches four distribution avenues: Apple, Barnes & Noble Press, Kobo, and Google Play Books. Let's discuss each Amazon alternative now.

# AMAZON ALTERNATIVE #1:
# APPLE BOOKS FOR AUTHORS

**WEBSITE:** AUTHORS.APPLE.COM

**DISTRIBUTION:** ARGENTINA, AUSTRALIA, AUSTRIA, BELGIUM, BOLIVIA, BRAZIL, BULGARIA, CANADA, CHILE, COLOMBIA, COSTA RICA, CYPRUS, CZECH REPUBLIC, DENMARK, DOMINICAN REPUBLIC, ECUADOR, EL SALVADOR, ESTONIA, FINLAND, FRANCE, GERMANY, GREECE, GUATEMALA, HUNGARY, HONDURAS, IRELAND, ITALY, JAPAN, LATVIA, LITHUANIA, LUXEMBOURG, MALTA, MEXICO, NETHERLANDS, NEW ZEALAND, NICARAGUA, NORWAY, PANAMA, PARAGUAY, PERU, POLAND, PORTUGAL, ROMANIA, SLOVAKIA, SLOVENIA, SPAIN, SWEDEN, SWITZERLAND, UNITED KINGDOM, UNITED STATES, AND VENEZUELA

---

Apple Books for Authors recently underwent a major facelift and rebranding, now offering distribution in over fifty-one countries and regions.[ii] Even Amazon doesn't cover some of those areas, making Apple a wise choice for reaching a broader global audience with your ebook or audiobook.

You can publish ebooks on Apple with an epub file. It's that simple. You can literally use the same metadata as you'd use on other platforms. Publishing ebooks on Apple originally was available only to those with a Mac. Now anyone with internet access can publish their work on the platform.

Audiobooks are a bit more problematic. Currently, Apple does not accept any direct submissions. The solution? Publish your audiobook on other approved partners like Findaway Voices, or even their competitors in ACX, and you can get audiobook distribution on Apple. Seem crazy? Well, not so much if you realize how much work goes into vetting poor-quality audiobooks. Rather than building the team and infrastructure to support publishing audiobooks, Apple merely allows a third-party to weed out the undesirables before a book ever makes it to their platform.

One exception to the rule for direct audiobook distribution comes through Apple's digital narration service.[iii] This free service allows account holders to produce audiobooks narrated by artificial intelligence (AI). You still keep the audiobook rights, so should you want to distribute different versions of your book elsewhere, you can.

While I'm not the biggest fan of AI-narrated content, some listeners don't mind it. If you don't like what Apple offers in digital narration, then that's no big deal. Move on. I still recommend keeping a close eye on Apple and asking anyone who has sold audiobooks on the platform about their experience.

> *Fun fact: Did you know Apple doesn't recognize ACX as a preferred partner? In fact, Apple pays a 25% to 40% royalty per sale on audiobooks distributed through ACX. By comparison, Apple's preferred partners like Findaway Voices by Spotify earn 45% of every sale made through Apple.*

If you're interested in publishing ebooks on Apple, you will earn 70% of every sale, regardless of the purchase price listed on their platform. KDP penalizes authors who price their ebook outside of

$2.99 and $9.99 by paying authors a much lower royalty rate of 35%. The Amazon sweet spot is between $2.99 and $9.99, where you earn the highest royalties.

Apple doesn't base royalties on the book's purchase price. They allow you to price your ebook however you want and pay you the same rate no matter the amount of the sale. Amazon should take note; more authors might be receptive to publishing exclusively on KDP if they stopped forcing authors to choose between the 35% and 70% royalty. That's yet another reason authors should consider publishing wide.

Apple likewise does not charge delivery fees for ebooks. Most authors don't realize that KDP charges delivery fees for each ebook sold via the 70% royalty model. Should you switch to the 35% royalty model, you don't have to pay the fees, but then again, they already take half your payout. Apple doesn't charge extra delivery fees for ebooks. Unlike shipping fees for print books, delivery fees for ebooks are charges for sending the digital file to customers.

Apple processes payments 45 days after each month. For example, they pay January sales on March 15 and February sales on April 15. To receive payment, you must submit your banking and tax information and meet the minimum threshold. In the US, Apple pays earnings over $0.02, while other regions require a minimum of $50. To see what your region allows, visit their website covering Apple Books Payments.[iv]

> *Quick tip: If you're in a region where a distributor doesn't honor your bank account, use a service called Payoneer. It works similar to PayPal, yet functions more like a bank account.*

Along with pricing and fee advantages, Apple doesn't require exclusivity, allowing you to publish your ebook wherever and whenever you choose.

The user interface for Apple Books for Authors can be confusing at first. You'll need to create an Apple ID and set up payment information through iTunes Connect. However, once you learn where everything is, it becomes easier with practice. When uploading to Apple for the first time, give yourself extra time to figure things out. As with any wide publishing platform, don't wait until the last minute to explore it. Review each account thoroughly before you're ready to publish—I'd hate for you to realize too late that publishing on the platform is more challenging than expected.

# AMAZON ALTERNATIVE #2:
# BARNES & NOBLE PRESS

**WEBSITE:** HTTPS://PRESS.BARNESANDNOBLE.COM
**DISTRIBUTION:** US ONLY

---

Barnes & Noble Press (B&N) is a mixed bag for self-publishers looking to expand their reach, but it comes with one significant limitation—distribution. I know it seems crazy that I recommend you publish to a platform with limited reach, but it's for good reason. While B&N only sells within the US, what they offer is exceptional.

On B&N Press, you can distribute ebooks, a whole variety of print books, and, to a certain extent, audiobooks. Having so many options in one place is rather convenient, especially if you want high quality print-on-demand options. On the disappointing side of things, formatting your print content is a pain if you're not familiar with graphic design tools. Rather than providing print files with RGB coloring, B&N requires CMYK. This is for good reason: The print quality comes out noticeably better. But this can be a challenge for inexperienced self-publishers.

Anyone planning to use the same print files on B&N that they used on KDP is in for a rude awakening. B&N has strict specifications for their print books. If you want to skirt past their vetting process for print books, look into alternative means of distribution to B&N (i.e., Draft2Digital, IngramSpark, KDP Expanded Distribution). I recommend directly uploading to B&N so you can compare the difference in quality compared to B&N's competitors. B&N hardcover books and hardcovers with dust jackets are premium quality. I'm hard-pressed to recommend any other platform that can produce the consistent and reliable quality of B&N Press.

On B&N Press, you'll get a far better print quality than other third-party options. Admittedly, I use IngramSpark to distribute print books to B&N because I don't see the value of directly uploading simply for a better cut or print quality. I feel IngramSpark's print-on-demand quality is comparable to B&N. This tracks because B&N uses Lightning Source, a sister company to IngramSpark, for print fulfillment.

> *Side note: Ingram Book Group manages print distribution for companies like IngramSpark, Lightning Source, Draft2Digital, Lulu's Global Distribution, and KDP's Expanded Distribution.*

Another minor inconvenience comes with publishing audiobooks. Sadly, there's no direct way to publish your audiobooks on their platform. You must use alternative resources like Findaway Voices by Spotify to distribute your audiobooks to B&N. I imagine B&N has the same reasons for blocking direct publishing of audiobooks as Apple. Audiobook quality management requires a dedicated team and complex infrastructure. Rather than investing in all that, B&N

relies on approved third-party companies to provide decent quality audiobooks.

B&N's royalty structure is straightforward for ebooks, with a 70% royalty regardless of sales price, and pricing is limited to $0.99 to $199.99. I prefer this approach—why penalize authors for pricing their books according to their value? It's beyond me why KDP doesn't follow suit with their competitors.

If you publish print books through any company using Ingram Book Group, then the book will appear on the B&N retail platform. B&N Press will summarily reject your publication since they don't want duplicate published books on their platform. Contact customer support for extra guidance.

Should you decide to give B&N Press print books a shot, the royalties are fairly modest, yet comparable to the other platforms. You'll earn a royalty of 55% minus the print costs, which varies based on the number of pages. The more pages your book has, the more the print cost will increase. An example B&N provides is:

- Suggested Retail Price = $13.99
- Retail & Distribution Cost = $6.30
- Author Royalty = $7.69 (55% royalty)
- Printing Cost = $4.57
- Net Author Profit = $3.12

B&N Press bases this example on a six- by nine-inch paperback with 300 pages in black and white. Should you choose more premium options like full color or hardcover, the base print fees will increase substantially. This isn't unusual, because all print-on-demand distributors charge more for color printing and hardcover options.

You can shop around, but most choices offer limited options, often forcing you to raise your sales price to turn a profit.

Since you cannot directly publish your audiobook through B&N Press, I can't give you a specific royalty per sale. Based on the agreement between B&N and the third-party distributor, the royalty rate can vary. You'll learn more about royalties for audiobooks distributed through third parties in a future chapter and can use that to estimate the range of royalties you might earn if those platforms sell your audiobook on B&N.

Barnes & Noble pays thirty days after the close of the month if you meet a $10 threshold. If your earnings are below that, they will pay you bi-annually. There are no additional hidden fees from B&N, and they make the payout system simple to navigate. Provide your bank account info (both US and international). If you don't have a supported bank account, consider a service like Payoneer.

Once you get past the steep learning curve of publishing print-on-demand books through Barnes & Noble Press, it's smooth sailing. While I use this platform primarily for ebooks, I have dabbled with print books with moderate success. Give B&N Press a shot. You might surprise yourself!

# AMAZON ALTERNATIVE #3: KOBO WRITING LIFE

**WEBSITE:** KOBO.COM/US/EN/P/WRITINGLIFE

**DISTRIBUTION:** AUSTRALIA, BRAZIL, CANADA, FRANCE, ITALY, JAPAN, MEXICO, NETHERLANDS/BELGIUM, NEW ZEALAND, PHILIPPINES, PORTUGAL, SPAIN, TURKEY, USA. KOBO WRITING LIFE REACHES OVER 190 COUNTRIES.

---

Kobo Writing Life (KWL) is a company owned by the publicly traded corporation Rakuten. With a focus on ebooks and audiobooks, KWL has some of the best user interfaces and customer service systems in self-publishing today. Even if you are brand new to publishing, KWL makes it super easy and fairly intuitive to publish on their platform—with one limitation. Kobo does not distribute print books. But they have some advantages for ebooks and audio, so let's get into the specifics.

Unlike their competitors, KWL allows direct publishing of audiobooks. Admittedly, I have yet to tap into the option since I use Findaway Voices by Spotify for distribution on Kobo. I plan to try it soon.

For ebooks, KWL distributes to fourteen regions through twenty-two regional partners. However, KWL states that while these regions are accessible, they do not guarantee distribution. According to KWL:

> *There will be certain factors, however, such as the language, which may prevent the books from being distributed through these channels.*[v]

In a live interview on the Kobo Writing Life YouTube channel, I pressed the Director of KWL, Tara Cremin, on the lack of print options on this platform. As of this publication, KWL only handles ebooks and audiobooks because they feel their resources and time are best spent on making their current options better while allowing other companies to handle print-on-demand. A lack of print distribution is not a deal breaker for me.

## OVERDRIVE: LIBRARY DISTRIBUTION THROUGH KOBO WRITING LIFE

You will notice two unique options when publishing your ebook through KWL: OverDrive and the Kobo Plus program. OverDrive is a library distribution partner, which is a very appealing option for many authors. Unlike Amazon, OverDrive supplies ebooks to libraries for stocking on their virtual shelves. OverDrive doesn't guarantee placement in libraries; you'll need to do the legwork by asking libraries to stock your book, or local patrons will need to request that their library order it. At least, however, OverDrive gives you the opportunity to get your ebook in the library's catalogue—and that means potentially reaching tens of thousands of library readers throughout the US and beyond.[vi]

Setting your book's price on OverDrive is separate—and generally should be higher—from the regular ebook purchase price. This model is called One Copy/One User (OCOU). Since more library patrons are going to read your one book than if one person bought it for themselves, most industry experts recommend pricing a book that will be available for library distribution at least two to three times the normal retail price. The higher price reflects the value of a single ebook in a library, accounting for the many readers who can access it through OverDrive.

OverDrive pays you 50% of your library price (for OCOU) and does not charge any aggregator fees like you would with Draft2Digital or Streetlib. This deal is unmatched anywhere else. It's a *huge* reason I love Kobo Writing Life so much; they distribute your book to OverDrive at no additional cost.

That's not the only way OverDrive pays. If you are an author who expects a high volume of library borrowers to want your book, then being paid two to three times the sales price will not compensate you for the expected volume of readers. Instead of the OCOU model, OverDrive allows authors to make their books available to libraries on a Cost Per Circulation (CPC) basis. Unfortunately, the author can't choose the compensation model; that decision is up to the library.

Let's say a library wants to purchase your book and instead of paying once for the book (the higher OCOU price), that library pays authors on a CPC basis. That means instead of a one-time purchase of your title for unlimited borrows of your book, the library will pay you 10% of your OCOU price every time a patron checks out your ebook.

> *Pro tip: …(A) quarter of all OverDrive sales are driven by reader requests…(Let) your readers know your books are available on OverDrive so they can request them from their local libraries!*[vii]

## KOBO PLUS: THE KDP SELECT ALTERNATIVE

If KDP Select hasn't delivered the results you expected, the Kobo Plus program might be worth considering. Subscribers of Kobo Plus pay a flat monthly fee to read an unlimited number of books available in the program. KWL pays authors based on a revenue share model similar to the KDP compensation pool. The Kobo Plus subscriptions from the month go into a pool to be paid out to authors based on minutes read. It's a fairly complex compensation structure unless you break down the math behind it. What you need to know is that KWL pays 60% of gross profits earned from Kobo Plus.

In an example, KWL shared these numbers:

- 100 subscribers at $9.99/month = $999 in the pool
- Subscribers average 2 hours reading per day for the month = 360,000 hours
- $999 ÷ 360,000 = $0.0027 (value per minute consumed)[viii]
- 2 hours read x $0.0027 = $0.0054
- $0.0054 x 60% compensation rate to authors= $0.0032 earned

Now, that's merely an example and not necessarily how much you'll actually get paid. You might have over two hours read, so your paycheck will be significantly more. Rather than give you a best-case scenario and set your expectations high, I figure it's best to show you how little it can pay you. As Kobo Plus continues to expand its reach to other regions, you might notice a bump in earnings. The only way to know is to distribute directly through Kobo Writing Life so you can take advantage of Kobo Plus.

The biggest difference between Kindle Unlimited (KU) and Kobo Plus for authors is that KWL does not require exclusivity and even encourages publishing beyond their platform. KWL seems to have the author's best interests at heart and understands that limiting authors to one platform can stifle reach.

For those of you concerned about cannibalizing ebook profits by enrolling in Kobo Plus, fear not! Just like many KU readers primarily read books included in their subscription, readers who buy the Kobo Plus subscription may not be the same type of customers who would buy the ebook—especially those written by new-to-them authors. By making your book available at no additional cost to Kobo Plus readers, you're distributing your book to a different customer.

I always recommend giving subscription-based distribution a shot—especially since Kobo Plus does not require exclusivity. If it doesn't pan out for you and you disagree with my philosophy, you can always remove it from the Kobo Plus program and be no worse off.

As for outright ebook royalties, you will earn 70% for every sale of an ebook priced above $2.99. You get a 45% royalty rate for anything priced below $2.99. Yes, the royalty structure is almost like KDP, except KWL pays you 10% more for pricing below $2.99. Unlike KDP, there's no maximum pricing level that puts your book back into a 45% royalty.

For audiobooks, you get 32% for subscription purchases or 45% for à la carte purchases at or above $2.99. For any pricing below that threshold, you'll earn only a 35% royalty.[ix] Before you shrug off Kobo Writing Life's audiobook distribution because of its modest royalty percentage, keep in mind that most audiobook distributors pay an average of 40% per sale. Sad, but true. I'm sure it has a lot to do with covering file hosting costs and staffing for moderation and vetting books. Compared to the 40% standard, KWL's 35% isn't significantly lower than the competition.

For ebook and audiobook pricing minimums per region on Kobo Writing Life, be sure to check their Help Page. Though the US minimum is $2.99, other regions may have different minimums.

KWL pays forty-five days after the close of the month with a minimum royalty earned of $50. They honor most banks and will deliver via electronic funds transfer (EFT).

Kobo Writing Life is a breath of fresh air in the self-publishing business and continues to innovate their product line and expand their reach. If only they included print books, I'd feel more confident about going exclusive on their platform to see how it compares to the almighty Kindle Direct Publishing. Maybe in due time. For now, what they provide is superb!

# AMAZON ALTERNATIVE #4: GOOGLE PLAY BOOKS PARTNER CENTER

**WEBSITE:** PLAY.GOOGLE.COM/BOOKS/PUBLISH

**DISTRIBUTION:** ARGENTINA, AUSTRALIA, AUSTRIA, BAHRAIN, BELARUS, BELGIUM, BOLIVIA, BRAZIL, CANADA, CHILE, COLOMBIA, COSTA RICA, CZECH REPUBLIC, DENMARK, DOMINICAN REPUBLIC, ECUADOR, EGYPT, EL SALVADOR, ESTONIA, FINLAND, FRANCE, GERMANY, GREECE, GUATEMALA, HONDURAS, HONG KONG, HUNGARY, INDIA, INDONESIA, IRELAND, ITALY, JAPAN, JORDAN, KAZAKHSTAN, KUWAIT, KYRGYZSTAN, LATVIA, LEBANON, LITHUANIA, LUXEMBOURG, MALAYSIA, MEXICO, NETHERLANDS, NEW ZEALAND, NICARAGUA, NORWAY, OMAN, PANAMA, PARAGUAY, PERU, PHILIPPINES, POLAND, PORTUGAL, QATAR, ROMANIA, RUSSIA, SAUDI ARABIA, SINGAPORE, SLOVAKIA, SOUTH AFRICA, SOUTH KOREA, SPAIN, SWEDEN, SWITZERLAND, TAIWAN, THAILAND, TURKEY, UKRAINE, UNITED ARAB EMIRATES, UNITED KINGDOM, UNITED STATES, URUGUAY, UZBEKISTAN, VENEZUELA, VIETNAM[x]

---

The biggest concern authors run into when going wide is the actual reach. While some platforms tap into maybe a dozen markets, Google Play Books Partner Center (GPB) reaches over seventy-five different regions and countries. By far, GPB has the widest reach of the Amazon alternatives. This reach includes ebook and audiobook, but at this time—like KWL—they have no stated plans for print book distribution.

One benefit of publishing through GPB is you'll tap into the world's most used search engine today: Google. When publishing an ebook through GPB, Google indexes the sample content used on the product page. Having your book indexed on Google makes your brand more discoverable and increases your likelihood of reaching more readers while selling more books. The best part is that you can control how much of your book appears in the sample.

As an example, I published my ebook, *The Chest & Arms Workout Plan,* through GPB. Making the title free opened a floodgate of new readers. Any time someone searched "chest and arms workout" through Google, my title came up on the first page of search results. That was *huge*. Publishing my ebook as free brought in way more readers, email subscribers, and devoted followers who bought more of my fitness books.

Is this a strategy you could use for your ebook on GPB? Possibly, it just depends on how much of a backlog you have. Anyone new to publishing shouldn't consider pricing your books as free until you have at least six or more titles beyond the free one.

With GPB, you can price your ebook however you want and will earn a 70% royalty for every sale[xi]. No catch, no asterisk, no shenanigans. GPB doesn't even charge delivery fees, unlike Kindle Direct Publishing. I can confidently say while Amazon reaches a massive customer base, the audience you reach through Google Play Books is still rather significant. That's enough for you to at least consider the value of publishing books through them. You reach a wide audience beyond Amazon, get paid a little better, and control your pricing however you like.

Recently, GPB opened audiobook publishing, giving authors a direct pipeline to the Google Play Books marketplace. Previously, if you wanted your audiobook distributed to Google Play Books, you had to use a third-party company like Findaway Voices by Spotify. Now you can go direct, cutting out any intermediary who'd eat into your total profits.

GPB offers a 52% royalty for audiobook sales, which is 12% higher than the exclusive ACX rate and 27% more than selling on a non-exclusive basis through ACX. You'll just have to provide your audio files, and GPB handles the rest. The only problem you'll run into is finding a narrator and producing your audiobook since GPB doesn't manage that.

However, like Apple Books for Authors, GPB has a built-in digital narration feature where AI will produce your audio files. GPB even encourages account holders to use those files in distribution elsewhere if they'd like, with no exclusivity requirement.

Google pays authors on the fifteenth day after the close of the month. Their payout model is the fastest option. They pay through wire transfer or electronic funds transfer (EFT) to your bank. Wire transfers require a minimum $100 threshold for payment, while EFTs only need $1 in earnings before paying out.

The Google Play Books dashboard still needs a little work, but they have come a long way over the past few years. I'll give credit where it's due, especially since GPB has brought me a fair chunk of change from book sales.

In 2019, GPB rolled out a new feature for publishing ebooks to their platform. Authors could no longer go through aggregate publishers like PublishDrive without allowing the third-party companies permission to access your GPB account. Sure, they won't see your sensitive, personal information, but you're giving another party access to an account you already have access to. To be honest, uploading to Google Play Books is a cinch, so having another company do it for you simply to take a percentage of your profit every month makes no sense.

We'll cover how to upload your manuscript in the chapter on *Wide Publishing for eBooks*. If you can manage it, go direct with Google Play Books. Should you find the steps to be a bit much, then consider aggregate publishers to manage your uploads. Aggregate publishing is a highly effective way of getting distribution to inaccessible avenues, so I won't fault you for allowing others to manage your assets if it means saving a little time. Let's explore aggregate publishing and why it plays an integral role in publishing wide.

# CHAPTER 3:
# AGGREGATE PUBLISHING

Quite a few experienced self-publishers recommend uploading directly to all platforms yourself and avoiding aggregate publishing companies. Their belief is that authors earn the highest royalties possible while cutting out any go-between who would share in the profits. Aggregate publishers act as intermediaries by distributing your book across multiple platforms for you. How you and the company earn profits from your book sales gets tricky.

You'll find three types of business models available through aggregate publishers:

1. Revenue share
2. Upfront payment
3. Subscriptions

Most popular aggregate publishers use a revenue share model, taking a percentage of the profits from royalties earned on books they distribute.

However, just because an aggregate publisher sells your book doesn't guarantee you all the profits. First, each platform takes their cut.

Then they send the remaining balance to the aggregator, who then takes their percentage. That leaves you with what's left after both companies have deducted their portion.

For newbie authors, the revenue share model may feel totally fine since you're only missing out on an average of 15% of the net profit. Of course, check each aggregate publisher's guidelines to determine the actual percentage they charge.

Rather than having a middleman take out a portion of your revenue, you may prefer paying one lump sum for an aggregate publisher to distribute your book. (See BookBaby.) Under that compensation model, you take all the risk upfront but get all the rewards on the back end. After paying the aggregate publisher a fee up front, you keep 100% of net profits. The biggest issue here comes if you need to update your manuscript. Should you find any problems or need to adjust anything, you'll have to pay another lump sum to the aggregator to update or upload another version of your book. With platforms like KDP, you pay nothing for updating your work.

Some aggregate publishers compensate authors through a subscription-based model. (See PublishDrive.) The company charges you a monthly fee based on how many books you publish through them. New authors should proceed with caution. In order to make back your monthly investment, you need to at least consider how many books you need to sell to break even. It's a tough decision since you can't really predict whether you'll actually sell the minimum number of books.

Much like the upfront payment model, subscription-based publishing allows you to collect 100% of net profits. For example, if you use PublishDrive for distribution and you select their Starter subscription, you pay $13.99 per month to publish three books forever—or for as long as you use the publishing aggregator. Assuming you price your ebook at $9.99 and make two sales on Apple Books through PublishDrive, then you'd earn $6.99 per sale based on Apple's 70% royalty. By making only two sales per month, you'll cover the $13.99 subscription fee and have a few bucks in profit left over.

Is it risky to pay for aggregate publishing? Sure, because it's on you to produce results consistently and get more book sales. Once they publish your work, the only task they have is to gather all the sales data from each avenue, collect the money, then deliver it to you. No revenue comes out of your check since you already pay monthly subscription fees.

Is there ever a right time to pay an aggregate publisher to distribute your books? I spoke with a newbie author who's in college. He wanted to publish his book but didn't have the time to figure out formatting, cover design, distribution, and a few other things. Fortunately for him, he had the discretionary budget to invest in BookBaby's services. Yes, it cost him about $3,000 upfront, but the service included many benefits. The biggest advantage he found was that he had less work to get his book published.

With PublishDrive's subscription model at $13.99 per month for distributing three books, it would take 300 months to match the $3,000 upfront cost of a lump-sum model. With BookBaby, he spent the $3,000 and then no longer needs to spend money on the company unless he wants specific updates or upsells.

Why even bother having an intermediary? Isn't that going to take away from your bottom line? Yes, but consider the amount of work it requires publishing on every single platform. An aggregate publisher removes the friction for authors for a nominal fee. But it goes so much deeper than that, as you'll soon discover.

## WHY YOU SHOULDN'T CUT OUT THE MIDDLEMAN

With Amazon KDP, Apple Books for Authors, Barnes & Noble Press, Kobo Writing Life, and Google Play Books, you're easily going to spend an hour uploading content to each of the different platforms. Now, if you want to publish beyond these sites, add even more time to your publishing schedule. Not to mention if you ever need to update your manuscript, you'll have to visit each site to upload the new version.

These small time drains gradually pull you away from your primary focus: writing, publishing new content, or promoting your backlog.

Aggregate publishing saves you precious time while getting access to other avenues unreachable to indie authors. When you have to update a manuscript, you only go through one dashboard instead of six or more. You'll also find tracking sales, expenses, and tax forms much easier when you have one dashboard to work on.

The greatest disadvantage to using aggregate publishing is that you don't have as much control over customizing metadata. While you did your best to optimize keywords in your metadata for discovery on Amazon, it does not mean it'll work the same on platforms outside of the online retail juggernaut. Is this a deal breaker? For me, no, but others who have strong Type A personalities might not like the lack of control.

You do retain control over your content and a generalized approach to metadata, so focus on killer ad copy for your book description. After all, if your book isn't as discoverable because of a lack of customized metadata, you can at least make the most of the traffic you get by crafting a book description that converts regardless of the platform.

Should you find that one platform performs really well through an aggregator, you can always do a quick search for direct publishing options. The worst thing that can happen is you cannot get direct access onto that platform so you continue to use the aggregator.

Thankfully, I have eliminated the guesswork on which avenues pull the best sales beyond KDP (i.e., Apple, B&N, Kobo, Google Play Books). Other avenues outside of these can be a mixed bag. Sure, you might have great sales through some random distributor in China, but that's likely the exception to the rule. Most authors earn very little revenue beyond the five platforms I mentioned. You might as well allow an aggregator to distribute everywhere and anywhere on your behalf and let them take a slight cut through a revenue share.

Let's explore some of the best aggregate publishing options and discuss what you can expect from each.

# AGGREGATE PUBLISHER #1:
## DRAFT2DIGITAL

**WEBSITE:** DRAFT2DIGITAL.COM

**DISTRIBUTION:** AMAZON, BARNES & NOBLE, KOBO (INCLUDING KOBO PLUS), APPLE BOOKS, TOLINO, VIVLIO, SMASHWORDS, GARDNERS, FABLE, EVERAND, OVERDRIVE, ODILO, CLOUDLIBRARY, BAKER & TAYLOR, HOOPLA, BORROWBOX, AND PALACE MARKETPLACE

---

Draft2Digital (D2D) is a company established *by* indie authors *for* indie authors. They currently distribute ebooks and paperbacks, and they integrate with audiobook publisher Findaway Voices by Spotify.

### DRAFT2DIGITAL EBOOKS

This aggregate publisher uses a revenue share model where they take 10% of the retail cost for each book sale. As an example, D2D will take $0.99 of an ebook sold for $9.99. Remember, all online retailers have different royalty agreements in place with Draft2Digital, so your cut is going to vary per platform. For example, if you sell an ebook distributed by D2D, Barnes & Noble pays a 70% royalty per sale, which goes to D2D as the aggregate publisher. Then D2D takes 10% of the retail cost of your book from the amount paid to them by B&N. You receive the remaining royalty directly from D2D.

## DRAFT2DIGITAL PRINT BOOKS

For print books, D2D offers distribution through Ingram Book Group, which reaches over 40,000 online retailers, libraries, and bookstores. You can publish your book in one of six trim sizes, with black ink, and only in paperback. You'll earn a 45% royalty minus the base print cost. This is significant because the Ingram base print costs are 15% lower than KDP's paperback books (5% higher than KDP's Expanded Distribution).

> *Side note: KDP's Expanded Distribution uses part of the same network as D2D, but only in the US and UK. In contrast, D2D taps into the full reach of Ingram Book Group, not just the US and UK, making it the wider option for paperback distribution through that channel.*

## DRAFT2DIGITAL PAYMENTS

D2D pays on or around the 15th day of each month. They further state:

> *Our partners all have different policies on payment timing. Most stores pay authors 60-90 days after the sale happens.*[xii]

The options for receiving payments from D2D are the most robust across all self-publishing, including:

- PayPal = $0 USD minimum
- Direct deposit = $0 USD minimum
- International Direct Deposit = $20 USD minimum
- Payoneer = $20 USD minimum
- Check = $100 USD minimum

## OTHER NOTABLE FACTS ABOUT DRAFT2DIGITAL

There are many reasons to publish through D2D, but the biggest two advantages include their free interior formatting tool and their Books2Read Universal Book Link Service.

If you can't afford professional interior formatting or don't have time to learn complex software like Adobe InDesign, D2D's free interior formatting tool is an excellent alternative. Though it doesn't function as a word processor, you can upload your manuscript as a .doc, .docx, .RTF, or .epub file. Then, in the preview phase of the upload process, D2D provides basic templates based on specific themes and niches. Sure, you can't adjust minor details in the dashboard, but you can certainly tweak elements in your original manuscript and re-upload it to get the template to work for your project just right.

The Books2Read (B2R) service provides free universal book links. You essentially share any product page URL from any platform for your ebook on the B2R link generator and press search. Then the service searches the internet for all findable links to your ebook. Fair warning: B2R won't uncover all links. You will have to hunt down the paperback, hardcover, and audiobook iterations for each retailer, then save the link in B2R. B2R then generates a single universal link that lets readers choose from a list of options, including various regions, to find your book on their preferred platform. Even if you publish only on Amazon, using a B2R link removes most of the friction for potential readers.

Most authors share the link to their book that's specific to one region. When a potential customer visits that link from outside the region-specific URL, they won't be able to order your book. With

B2R links, customers can select the region they buy from and choose the store they prefer.

To make matters even easier, D2D does not require you to publish through their platform to use these two tools. It's a big win for you, the author! If you're ever wondering if D2D is a good fit or you need questions answered, contact their Support team. They're second to none.

With the universal book links, interior formatting, and the sleek, modern user interface, Draft2Digital is the go-to resource for aggregate publishing your books. I cannot recommend them highly enough. Do yourself a favor and give them a shot. I believe in D2D so much that I have a referral link that you're welcome to use ([DaleLinks.com/D2D](DaleLinks.com/D2D)). I genuinely recommend this service to self-publishers regardless of any personal benefit, though I do earn a small commission if you use my referral link.

# AGGREGATE PUBLISHER #2:
# INGRAMSPARK

**WEBSITE:** INGRAMSPARK.COM

**DISTRIBUTION:** OVER 40,000 INDEPENDENT BOOKSTORES, EBOOK RETAILERS, ONLINE STORES, LIBRARIES, CHAIN STORES, AND UNIVERSITIES THROUGHOUT THE WORLD.

**EBOOK DISTRIBUTION INCLUDES:** AINOSCO, AMAZON*, APPLE**, BARNES & NOBLE NOOK, CLOUDLIBRARY, BIBLIU, BOLINDA, BOOKTOPIA, CHEGG, DE MARQUE, EBOOKS.COM, EBSCO, FABLE, FINDAWAY, FOLLETT/B&T, GARDNERS, GLOSE, HOOPLA, HUMMINGBIRD, IGROUP, ITSI, KOBO PLUS, KORTEX, LEGIBLE, LIBREKA, LIBRI GMBH, LIBRO.FM, MACKIN, ODILO, OVERDRIVE, PERLEGO, PERUSALL, PROQUEST, REDSHELF, SCRIBD, SNAPPLIFY, STORYTEL, TAKEALOT, VITALSOURCE, WHEELERS, WOOK, YOUSCRIBE.

---

*If you're already distributing your ebook to Amazon, IngramSpark will bypass this avenue.

**IngramSpark distributes ebooks to Apple but can't if you publish your ebook through another third-party company. Unlike Amazon though, IngramSpark requires you to choose either IngramSpark or Apple distribution, not both. This means companies like Apple Books for Authors, Draft2Digital, PublishDrive, Streetlib, and more are out of the question for distributing your ebook to Apple.

IngramSpark is a self-publishing company founded in 2013 that distributes ebooks and a variety of print book options. This aggregate publisher has massive reach but comes with its share of pros and cons based on how you choose to use them.

For print books, IngramSpark reaches:

- United States & Canada: Retailers, Libraries, Schools, E-commerce companies, Amazon, Barnes & Noble, Independent bookstores, Walmart.com, and Chapters/Indigo (Canada).
- United Kingdom & Europe: Adlibris, Agapea, Amazon.co.uk, Aphrohead, Blackwell, Books Express, Coutts Information Services Ltd, Designarta Books, Eden Interactive Ltd, Foyles, Gardners, Trust Media Distribution (formerly STL), Mallory International, Paperback Shop Ltd, Superbookdeals, The Book Community Ltd, Waterstones, and Wrap Distribution.
- Australia & New Zealand: Amazon AU, Booktopia, Fishpond, The Nile, James Bennett, ALS, Peter Pal.

The parent company of IngramSpark, Ingram Book Group, handles distribution for a wide variety of print-on-demand platforms, such as KDP's Expanded Distribution, Draft2Digital, Lulu, Blurb, and more. In theory, their reach sounds impressive. When asked to list all 40,000 options in their distribution network, IngramSpark explains that privacy agreements with their partners prevent them from naming everyone.

IngramSpark provides a clear overview of the six major regions previously mentioned, but offers only vague information about distribution to China, South Korea, India, Japan, South Africa, and Brazil. Where do your books go in these regions? They won't disclose it—I've asked multiple times, to no avail.

Even though you might publish through an avenue available via Ingram Book Group, the retailers are not obligated to accept, display, or market your book. If Walmart.com doesn't see value in your title, they won't stock it, and Ingram can't force them to do it.

Understanding the royalty structure is where it gets hazy for some folks, so don't be too hasty to use IngramSpark. Yes, the platform is free to use—but this is a major change after operating for nearly a decade under a different model. Previously, authors had to pay an upload fee of $25 to $49 to use their platform and another $25 for any subsequent updates of your publication. On their tenth anniversary, IngramSpark celebrated by removing upload fees, but there was a catch. Account holders sacrifice 1% of every sale as a distribution fee, and any updates to the book cover or interior cost $25 after the first sixty days.

Try to complete any changes within the first two months of a book's life cycle to avoid the update surcharge.

> *Side note: The Alliance of Independent Authors (ALLi) is a nonprofit organization for indie authors that currently offers its members many perks, one of which is one free update per month with IngramSpark. Get details in the Resources section of this book.*

## INGRAMSPARK EBOOKS

IngramSpark offers forty-two avenues including options mentioned previously like Apple, Barnes & Noble, Kobo Plus, and OverDrive, among many others that you could get through Draft2Digital or through direct publishing. The one exception is Amazon. IngramSpark will defer to Amazon's product listing on the retail website.

The royalty you will earn fluctuates based on the distribution partner. Since IngramSpark has negotiated those terms on behalf of all account holders, you will earn roughly 10% to 70% royalty per sale of your ebooks. Don't let that range dissuade you because the options they have for ebook distribution are fairly diverse.

For instance, they offer three retail models for ebooks:

1. One book, one sale: This is exactly what you think it is. A customer buys your ebook and owns the perpetual license. That model pays a 50% royalty for seventeen retailers and 70% for Kobo sales.
2. Unlimited subscription model: Readers can pay a monthly fee to access digital titles through a subscription service. A sale counts when a user reads or consumes at least 20% of a title. IngramSpark offers three subscription services where you earn a 70% royalty.
3. Shared pool model: Readers pay a monthly fee to access a subscription service, and that money goes into a shared revenue pool that pays out to pieces of the pie to authors. You will earn royalties ranging from 45% to 65% across four subscription services.

Then, IngramSpark offers three library models:

1. Single-user: One library patron can access your title at a time. Think of it like a normal library where there are

limited print copies on hand and only one reader can check out that book. You earn a 70% royalty for thirteen library distributors.

2. Three-user: This is essentially the same thing as the single-user model, but three times as much pay. You'll get three times your retail value when using this model. Even though they use a 70% royalty model for three library distributors, you're going to be paid 150% of that amount since three users have access to the book.

3. Pay-per-use model: Subscribers gain unlimited access to your ebook, with profits split evenly between you and the library distributor, Hoopla. However, you only earn a 10% royalty, which you then share with IngramSpark. As a fan of library distribution, I'm willing to accept that trade-off to reach more libraries. That said, my revenue from Hoopla through Draft2Digital has been modest over the years.

Last, IngramSpark has other institutional sales models that include:

1. Short-term loan model: Readers access a digital title for a 24-hour period, with no limit on how many can view it simultaneously. Each checkout counts as a sale. You earn a 25% royalty from three partners. Some library and institutional distributors, like EBSCO, Gardners, and ProQuest, use a mix of these models.

2. Three-user: Hey, remember the three-user model for libraries? Well, this is the same thing.

3. Non-linear lending model: Libraries buy a license that grants 325 uses of a digital title per year. Each use happens when a

reader reads, copies, or prints part of the title. After 325 uses, access stops until the next year unless the library purchases another license. You earn a 70% royalty multiplied by 120%.

I don't expect you to remember every detail and option because I've been following IngramSpark for years now and can't remember half of it. If these terms don't work for you, you can look into other avenues.

Full disclosure: I avoid using IngramSpark for distribution because I want more granular control over where my ebooks go. I'd rather have the freedom to choose where my books go so that I can hit some retail platforms through direct features, collecting all the royalties and not just some. However, don't let that stop you from trying them with your next book. I've heard of many authors happy with ebook distribution through IngramSpark.

Just because one avenue doesn't work for my business doesn't mean it can't work for yours. Think about your discretionary time and budget (for example, the update fees charged by IngramSpark), then decide if their ebook distribution is right for you.

## INGRAMSPARK PRINT BOOKS

The selection and quality of print books through IngramSpark is nearly unparalleled. The distribution is massive, and you even increase your likelihood of placement in brick-and-mortar bookstores (physical shops) as long as you provide a deep wholesale discount and enable returns. More on that soon.

IngramSpark has a ludicrous number of print options. It's so impressive that I could write an entire chapter—heck, scratch that, an entire book—on all they offer. Let's keep it simple, and I'll let you explore the options on their site when you have a few minutes.

IngramSpark offers paperback (perfect bound), hardcover (case laminate), and hardcover with dust jacket. They have two variations for hardcover books with dust jackets: a digital cloth cover or case laminate. The first dust jacket option is a flat matte cover with the image of a cloth cover—think like the old school library books. Option two lets you add a custom image to the cover, even if it clashes with the dust jacket. Keep in mind, the more features you use for your book, the higher the base cost will be.

A huge factor that will determine the base print cost involves the paper you choose. IngramSpark offers one of four paper types and four ink options: Black & White, Standard Color, Premium Color, or Ultra-Premium Color. I've purposely listed the print books and features in a specific order to display as good-better-best. The fancier the book, the more it'll cost.

One of the unique features offered by IngramSpark for print books is their flexible royalty model. You set the royalty based on six markets: US, UK, European Union, Canada, Australia, and the rest of the world in Global Connect. How you set the royalty is based on the wholesale discount you provide to retailers. Each avenue requires a minimum to maximum wholesale discount:

- US: 40% to 55% wholesale discount giving you a 45% to 60% royalty
- UK, Europe, Canada & Australia: 35% to 55% wholesale discount giving you a 45% to 65% royalty

- Canada & Global Connect: 30% to 55% wholesale discount, giving you a 45% to 70% royalty (the best print book royalty yet)

These royalties are not bad, but you have to still account for base print costs and a 1% distribution fee. Compared to KDP, IngramSpark can provide a higher royalty based on what you select for a wholesale discount.

To increase your likelihood of retail placement, IngramSpark encourages account holders to offer the deepest discount plus enable returns. That last item can be pretty risky because if a buyer returns your books, you pay the full refund. IngramSpark charges you the wholesale cost of the book along with shipping fees. While you earn royalties from book sales, a return could cause a chargeback that exceeds your earnings. If you do not have the means to pay for returns, I highly recommend disabling the option. Revisit it when you can better assume that potential exposure.

Conversely, you have less risk and more reward with IngramSpark's direct sales feature called Share & Sell. This program allows you to produce a basic one-book product page for your print publication. You will earn a hefty royalty for any sale through your Share & Sell landing page. IngramSpark deducts only the base print cost and a $3.50 distribution surcharge fee from that sale. The customer still pays shipping and taxes, but you net a larger chunk of revenue.

As of this writing, IngramSpark only offers Share & Sell in the US with plans to expand to the UK, Canada, and Australia next. I spoke with the IngramSpark team, and they said their mission is to roll out direct sales gradually to account holders worldwide and improve the model over time. They've even shared that multi-product pages could be an eventual option developed under this model.

## INGRAMSPARK PAYMENTS

IngramSpark pays account holders ninety days after the close of the month through direct deposit or PayPal.

## OTHER NOTABLE FACTS ABOUT INGRAMSPARK

Any author looking for just print books for themselves can lean on IngramSpark, because you don't have to distribute through them to upload your book and print copies. You'll pay for the base print costs and shipping of the number of copies you want, then it's up to you what you do with the books.

All US account holders have the option of receiving a free print ISBN from IngramSpark when you upload a book to the platform. While you won't own the ISBN and can't take it anywhere else, it certainly is one less expense or hassle for you to worry about. In the US, authors must purchase their ISBNs from Bowker and that can cost from $1.50 to $125 per ISBN (based on bulk ordering). If you need to save a few bucks and you live in the US, then use IngramSpark's free option. If you want to use your own ISBN later, you can delist the original title and publish a second edition with the new ISBN.

IngramSpark offers account holders the ability to set up pre-sales—making your book available to reserve before launch day. I have yet to test that feature because I've heard some serious issues with how reliable it is. Popular YouTuber Mandi Lynn shared a nightmare scenario about IngramSpark mishandling her book launch.[xiii]

Allegedly, IngramSpark pushed out the placeholder manuscript well ahead of the book launch date, giving the readers early access to an unfinished book that was only meant to hold a spot for a pre-sale. The mistakes forced her to finish her book hurriedly and manage any negative reaction from her readers.

If you launch a pre-sale, proceed with caution. Otherwise, IngramSpark is a fairly solid option for publishing ebooks and print books. Should IngramSpark not have what you want, you've got a few other options to consider.

# AGGREGATE PUBLISHER #3:
# BOOKVAULT

**WEBSITE:** BOOKVAULT.APP

**DISTRIBUTION:** AMAZON, GARDNERS, ALIBRIS, AND THE GREAT BRITISH BOOK SHOP

---

Bookvault is a UK-based print-on-demand company that, similar to IngramSpark, specializes in all kinds of print books. Unlike their contemporaries, though, Bookvault doesn't distribute ebooks or audiobooks, though they've teased about developing those options in the distant future. Despite the lack in ebook and audiobook distribution, they make up for that with print options and quality.

## BOOKVAULT PRINT BOOKS

It may seem like Bookvault is working at a disadvantage over their competition, but the four distribution options are wide reaching. Does Bookvault offer 40,000 retailers like Ingram Book Group? No, but Bookvault reaches some prominent distributors with fairly wide reach.

Bookvault offers six types of binding:

- Paperback (perfect bound)

- Hardcover (case bound) with or without a dust jacket
- Hardcover (with cloth) with or without a dust jacket
- Foil blocking
- Wire-o bound notebooks
- Saddle stitch and spiral bound

While these options seem solid, not all are available for distribution beyond the UK. Research Bookvault thoroughly before committing.

Similar to IngramSpark, the fancier the features on your book, the more the base print cost increases, and, to a certain extent, the fewer distribution options you can access beyond Bookvault's online storefront, The Great British Book Shop.

Bookvault is similar to IngramSpark in that you can set the wholesale discount for sales in the US, UK, and Europe. This discount ranges from 20% to 60%, giving you an astounding 40% to 80% royalty (minus print fees). Bookvault charges a 5% distribution fee. The Great British Book Shop (TGBBS) offers one of the best royalties on the market today—90%—giving you the biggest bang for your buck. Bookvault and TGBBS take 5% each, leaving you the remaining profits after the deduction of print costs.

I've seen the print quality from Bookvault's UK printers, and it's unmatched—no print-on-demand company comes close. In the US, however, their print quality is comparable to other providers. Bookvault clearly excels in the UK, and I hope to see that same exceptional quality expanding into the US and beyond in the future.

Before you get too excited about Bookvault, there are a couple of small catches. They have three account types that come with their own perks and hang-ups. The free tier gets you access to their platform, but you have to pay a one-time upload fee of £19.95 per book. On the second subscription plan, you pay £24.95 per month for a lower upload fee: £4.95 per book. Then, with their highest subscription tier, you pay £89.95 per month with no book upload fees.

Also, you'll need to bring your own ISBN, because Bookvault doesn't provide one for free like other platforms. I recommend visiting the International ISBN Agency to see where you can buy an ISBN in your region (DaleLinks.com/ISBN).

If you don't have the money to get your ISBN, you can still use Bookvault's direct sales option through Shopify, WooCommerce, Wix, Payhip, and their API. ISBNs aren't essential for direct sales, but they're still a good idea to have.

You make direct sales when you are the vendor for your books, not Amazon, Bookvault, or any other company. Why would you want to sell direct? You get 100% of the net profit after base print costs. Yep! Feel free to soil your pants now.

Will your direct sales page generate as much traffic as Amazon or Barnes & Noble? Probably not, but with effort in building awareness, you can benefit from buyers coming directly to you. The best part about Bookvault's direct sales is that you get paid immediately—no waiting!

## BOOKVAULT PAYMENTS

Bookvault pays for global distribution 90 days after each sale, and TGBBS sends payments around the 14th of each month. Bookvault uses direct deposit only.

## OTHER NOTABLE DETAILS ABOUT BOOKVAULT

Bookvault makes a solid effort at standing out from the competition. They're constantly iterating on their business and testing new features. They recently added a custom feature—sprayed edges. If you want the page edges of your print book to have a certain color or graphic on them, Bookvault can do it. As you can imagine, that's *not* a feature available for global distribution.

For the past year, Bookvault has teased authors with the prospect of publishing physical boxsets. No other print-on-demand company offers that, so when they roll that out, they'll be ahead of the pack in terms of unique product options.

# AGGREGATE PUBLISHER #4:
# PUBLISHDRIVE

**WEBSITE:** PUBLISHDRIVE.COM

**EBOOK DISTRIBUTION:** AMAZON, APPLE, BARNES & NOBLE, GOOGLE PLAY BOOKS, KOBO, KOBO PLUS, EVERAND, STORYTEL, BOOKMATE, DREAME, 24SYMBOLS, PERLEGO, BAKER & TAYLOR, OVERDRIVE, HOOPLA, ODILO, CLOUDLIBRARY, MACKIN, IREADER, TOLINO, CHINESE EBOOK STORES, GARDNERS, CIANDO, EMPIK GROUP, LAZYJOY, DIBOOK, EKONYV, MULTIMEDIA PLAZA, E-LETOLTES.

**PRINT DISTRIBUTION:** AMAZON, INGRAM GLOBAL DISTRIBUTION, CNPEREADING PLATFORM, REPRO INDIA.

**AUDIOBOOK DISTRIBUTION:** APPLE, AUDIBLE, GOOGLE PLAY, KOBO, OVERDRIVE, BOOKMATE, CNPEREADING, FINDAWAY, GARDNER, VOXA, LAZYJOY, STORYTEL, APPLE BOOKS DIGITAL NARRATION.

---

PublishDrive distributes ebooks, paperback books, and digital audiobooks, but it comes with a catch. While platforms like Draft2Digital and IngramSpark function on a revenue share model, PublishDrive lets you keep the net profits from every sale. Instead of the shared revenue, authors pay a monthly subscription fee for distribution.

Don't get me wrong, though. You will never earn 100% of every sale; the retailers first take their cut. For example, when Apple Books sells a copy of your book, they'll take 30% of the sale. PublishDrive pays you the remaining 70%. However, they deduct a monthly fee, which applies regardless of your earnings. You only have to make sure you're paying the monthly bill or you're going to be left without a place to host and distribute your book.

If you're a new author without a following, a monthly subscription is likely not the best investment. However, if you have an established readership or are generating significant sales through a specific retailer, you can either go direct to the source (e.g., Apple or Barnes & Noble) or use PublishDrive to manage all those retailers in one place.

Rather than damn myself with forever updating this book, I'll refer you to PublishDrive for monthly subscription prices and the perks that come at each level. Right now, they have an option where you can distribute one ebook for free. Beyond that, their four subscription plans range from $13.99 for three books to $83.99 for forty-eight books. You'll get a better deal if you subscribe to an annual plan versus a monthly plan.

*Side Note: One book on PublishDrive indicates only one iteration of a specific book. This means if you want to publish the ebook, print book and audiobook, that's three books.*

## PUBLISHDRIVE EBOOKS

Similar to Draft2Digital, you can select or disable distribution for any options, giving you so much more freedom than IngramSpark. Sure, it comes at a monthly cost, but at least you have some control and say over where your book ends up. Not to mention that you can easily track down and find your book online with PublishDrive's automated tracking tools.

Like the previously mentioned options, the royalty varies from one retail option to the other. This ranges from 25% to 70% and is largely based on four models:

1. Retailers. Each retail site takes a cut from the sale of your book, then gives PublishDrive the rest to disburse to you.
2. Subscription services. You place your ebook in a subscription-based service which allows readers to check out your book and you're compensated from a monthly revenue pool.
3. Library providers. The way a library lends your book varies based on the established agreement between PublishDrive and the library distributor. Refer to the explanation in the previous subchapter about how libraries work.
4. Regional stores. PublishDrive reaches unique regions and retailers that no other platform offers. For example, you can submit your book for consideration to China. Sure, the work needs to meet their rigid censorship guidelines, but at least it's one way to get your book into that country.

Despite the initial sticker shock from the subscription model, you'll find the user interface for PublishDrive to be dead simple. One screen guides you through the entire process of uploading your book. While I love how platforms like KDP and Draft2Digital have the upload process broken into three to four steps, PublishDrive's single page upload process removes the friction for account holders, requiring fewer clicks.

## PUBLISHDRIVE PRINT BOOKS

This company offers quite a few options for publishing paperback books through four different print-on-demand distributors. With that wider distribution comes additional hoops you'll need to jump through based on what you need printed and where. PublishDrive offers sixteen trim sizes for paperback books in black ink or full color. They offer fifty-pound white or cream paper and glossy or matte covers.

But what can you expect to make per sale of a paperback book through PublishDrive? As far as compensation is concerned, Amazon, CNPeReading Platform, and Repro India pay 50% minus base print costs. For comparison, through Ingram you're paid 45% minus print costs. The PublishDrive rates are fairly competitive, but you have to question if going direct with Amazon and Ingram might be the better option. The Amazon KDP royalty rate is 60%—which is 10% more than PublishDrive's rate. Through IngramSpark, you can adjust your print royalty as desired, without being limited to the 45% option.

The plus side of things is that you can come with an ISBN or PublishDrive will furnish you with one. Of course, you can only use that free ISBN through PublishDrive.

Recently, PublishDrive polled account holders about the demand for hardcover books, so I'm sure they'll develop this as an option. When that happens, check with PublishDrive about trim sizes, paper type, ink selection, and more.

One major gripe I have with their print option is that you can't order proof copies of your book until it's published. While the distribution is excellent and receiving most of my revenue monthly is great, it's frustrating not being able to check for errors in the physical book before it hits the market. Yes, they offer a decent digital proofing process, but it's not an accurate way to verify how the book looks in print before it goes live to customers.

## PUBLISHDRIVE AUDIOBOOKS

Unlike most aggregate publishers, PublishDrive distributes all three iterations of your book: ebook, paperback, and audio. And they partner with a lot of big players in the audiobook retail industry. Boasting thirteen different avenues, some with an expanded reach like OverDrive or Findaway, PublishDrive is an excellent choice.

The royalty rates paid by PublishDrive run between 25% to 60%. Audible tends to earn the lowest payout options through PublishDrive, while the higher royalty applies to distribution to China. If you're already considering wide publishing for audiobooks, then PublishDrive might be what you're looking for.

Just a friendly reminder: Your book sales should align with or exceed subscription costs on PublishDrive. Figure out the number of sales you need to keep using their platform without going into debt. If you compare PublishDrive's subscription model with the Findaway Voices 80/20 revenue share model, you'll earn 20% more by using PublishDrive. If that additional 20% is more than what you'd pay to use PublishDrive every month, you know it's a good fit. Just stay consistent with your sales and you'll be fine.

## PUBLISHDRIVE PAYMENTS

PublishDrive prepares sales reports around the 10th of the month, two months following the sale, with the payment deadline set for the end of that same month. For example, sales from May will report around July 10th and you should receive payment by the end of July.

There are exceptions to this rule, as Amazon and Ingram POD sales follow a four-month cycle. This means that if you sell a print book in January, you will receive payment in May.

PublishDrive allows you to set the minimum payment threshold between $5 and $10,000, with payment options including wire transfer, local bank transfer, check, PayPal, or Intercash.

## OTHER NOTABLE FACTS ABOUT PUBLISHDRIVE

PublishDrive is constantly iterating and improving what they offer authors, and it shows in a wide range of features and tools they continue to roll out. Their premium cloud-based tool, Abacus, helps publishers and authors manage royalties, track sales, and split royalties for a monthly fee. If you co-authored a book with someone, you can try out Abacus with the first book free. They charge an additional $2.99 per book every month.

PublishDrive also offers an array of book marketing options that include running price promotions, sending free review copies, running ads through Amazon, and more. Since they have a direct relationship with some retailers (i.e., Kobo and Apple), PublishDrive offers regular promotional opportunities to authors that sometimes cost the author nothing.

If you're on a limited budget, PublishDrive offers a free ebook and print book converter, which is a helpful feature given the monthly fee. While I haven't used their software, I've yet to hear any complaints about it. They introduced an AI-generated cover designer in 2024, which could be another valuable tool for authors. I've yet to explore this option, so proceed with caution.

PublishDrive recently introduced an AI-powered book metadata generator called Publishing Assistant that helps with title creation, generating book descriptions, and category and keyword selection. All you have to do is upload your manuscript and their Publishing Assistant gets to work. PublishDrive gives all account holders sixty free credits to use toward AI tools for your book. If you need more credits, you'll have to purchase them. From what I've seen so far, it's a pretty decent tool that'll remove a lot of work you'd otherwise put into crafting the best description for your book. Just remember that all AI-generated content needs the same attention to editing and proofing, so don't simply copy and paste what you've been given.

Last, PublishDrive wants authors to feel confident using their distribution services, so they offer a calculator ([calculator.publishdrive.com](calculator.publishdrive.com)) to compare earnings on PublishDrive with those on Draft2Digital and IngramSpark. If you're unsure whether PublishDrive is right for you, use their calculator; it'll tell you.

# AGGREGATE PUBLISHER #5:
# LULU

**WEBSITE:** LULU.COM

**EBOOK DISTRIBUTION:** AMAZON, APPLE, BARNES & NOBLE, KOBO, EVERAND, LIBRI, GARDNERS, AND THE LULU BOOKSTORE.

**PRINT DISTRIBUTION:** GLOBAL DISTRIBUTION (INGRAM), LULU BOOKSTORE AND LULU DIRECT.

---

Operating since 2002, Lulu is one of the oldest self-publishing companies on this list. They provide distribution for both ebooks and print, focusing strongly on high-quality print-on-demand products, including more than just books.

By adding direct sales as an option that provides authors with 100% royalties minus print fees, Lulu is an excellent print-on-demand company to lean on.

Unfortunately, they do not have audiobook distribution, which is a bummer. Using Lulu gets a little complex, so let's address their distribution options.

## LULU EBOOKS

Lulu reaches top retail platforms like Amazon, Apple, Barnes & Noble, and Kobo, making the 90/10 revenue split a strong option for authors. But the 90% isn't a straight and simple number. Lulu maintains separate royalty agreements with each retailer, so keep in mind you will earn 90% of the *net* profit from each platform.

For example, if Apple offers a 70% royalty on every ebook sale, with Lulu distributing your book to Apple, you'll earn 90% of the 70% Apple royalty rate. That means if your ebook costs a customer $10.00, Apple keeps $3.00. Then Lulu will pay you 90% of the remaining $7.00 which is $6.30. You lose out on Lulu's earnings of $0.70 on that sale by not going direct. Is that a big deal for you? If not, maybe Lulu is right up your alley.

If you're still unconvinced, they still apply the 90/10 revenue split for sales made through the Lulu Bookstore. Since they own that storefront, there's no go-between taking a cut. Here's where you win big! Using the previous example of the $10 ebook, when you sell direct from the Lulu storefront, you will earn $9 per sale.

Amazon loyalists often argue that Lulu doesn't have the same customer base volume. While that's true, consider this: If you put the same effort into promoting a Lulu Bookstore link as you would an Amazon link, you could earn $2 more per book, even with Amazon's 70% royalty rate, based on the previous example.

Oh, and there are no funny pricing shenanigans with Lulu. You price your ebook how you want, and they'll pay you the same royalty, no matter what. Does KDP offer this? No, and that's why I tell people, if you want to stay with Amazon and aren't exclusive, consider the Lulu Bookstore as an additional avenue.

Distribution for ebooks with Lulu comes with a catch, though. Sadly, there's a one-time $4.99 processing fee for each ebook distributed through Lulu. They have a content moderation team that'll vet your ebook to make sure it's market ready. Any time you need to update your book, there's no fee.

## LULU PRINT BOOKS

Lulu stands out with their wide selection of high-quality print options that include paperback, hardcover, and hardcover with dust jacket. Their books come in sixteen trim sizes and four color options:

1. Standard Black & White
2. Premium Black & White
3. Standard Color
4. Premium Color

They have three types of paper:

- 60# Uncoated cream paper
- 60# Uncoated white paper
- 80# Coated white paper

Covers are available in glossy or matte finish.

Lulu offers global distribution for their print books through Ingram Book Group, except for three trim sizes, the Premium Black & White color option, and the 80# coated white paper. This means you'll reach the same avenues as IngramSpark, Draft2Digital, Blurb, and, to a limited extent, KDP Expanded Distribution.

One substantial issue with Lulu is the base print cost. In a video series where I compared Lulu with the other major print-on-demand companies, I found Lulu charged nearly 60% more than their competitors. Is this substantial upcharge worth the high-quality print? That's entirely your call.

Since Lulu print books come at a rather high premium, you'll have to price your book accordingly. Their top-tier product like the hardcover book with dust jacket and premium color will have a steep base cost, forcing you to charge readers way more than if you would if you'd used other print-on-demand companies.

You earn an 80% royalty after printing fees for print books, with Lulu keeping the remaining 20%. This royalty structure is quite nice if you're making sales through the Lulu Bookstore. It's a different scenario through their Global Distribution where the retail platforms will take their cut before the profits reach you. As you probably sense by now, the royalty split is already pre-arranged through Ingram Book Group, much like the previous platforms using that avenue.

Should you want to take advantage of Global Distribution, you must order one print proof of your book. This rule is most likely put in place by Ingram Book Group, ensuring that people aren't just pumping out steamy piles of hot trash on their platform. That barrier of entry might be a deal-breaker for anyone on a limited budget and that's okay. Don't lose heart; you can still use Lulu for its bookstore and another option we haven't discussed yet called Lulu Direct, their direct sales feature.

Lulu Direct is a great option if you're craving a hefty payout. This direct sales tool integrates with Shopify, WooCommerce, and API. Using Lulu Direct means you're selling the books from your site and using Lulu only for print fulfillment. That allows Lulu to give authors one of the best royalties you'll see with print-on-demand books: 100% minus print fees. When a reader buys your book through your Lulu Direct shop, they pay the money to you. All you have to do is give Lulu Direct the money for printing and shipping, then the rest of the sale price is yours to keep.

For example, if you sell a 6x9 paperback book with 120 pages in standard black & white on 60# white paper, then the base cost for printing that book would be $4.56. If you charge $19.99 for the book, the net profit you will earn comes to $15.43. The customer pays the shipping costs at the time of purchase, which you pass along to Lulu to ship the book. You never have to manage any physical products, inventory, or returns/exchanges. Lulu oversees it all. The only catch is if you don't pay Lulu, they won't fulfill the order. Monitor the email inbox associated with your Lulu account. They'll typically notify you whenever a customer places an order.

Amazon sets a high bar with two-day shipping options, so customers want their products fairly quick. One thing that works against Lulu Direct is the shipping times. When buying from Lulu Direct, the customer has the option to choose premium shipping options to get the book faster. Is it ideal? No, but it's nearly impossible for any print-on-demand company to keep up with the breakneck pace that Amazon does while maintaining quality print books every time.

Lulu Direct offers more print options and higher earnings per sale compared to Amazon KDP. While you most likely will not see the same customer traffic on your website, you can make up for a lack of traffic in higher earnings per sale.

For a better understanding of print book costs, visit Lulu's Pricing Calculator (Lulu.com/pricing). They'll even provide free interior and custom cover templates according to what you select.

## LULU PAYMENTS

This company pays out less frequently compared to the other platforms. Lulu pays account holders forty-five days following the end of a quarter. The payment periods are:

- February 15 for sales in October, November and December
- May 15 for sales in January, February, and March
- August 15 for sales in April, May, and June
- November 15 for sales in July, August, and September

Even though the other companies withhold earnings for up to ninety days before paying out, you're at least receiving royalties monthly. I've spoken with the folks at Lulu and expressed how much I don't like the lack of frequency, so they're aware of it. Will they change this rule just because of me? Possibly not, but time will tell.

Lulu pays by check or PayPal with a minimum payment threshold of $5 and $20, respectively.[xiv] As mentioned previously, any sales made through Lulu Direct go right to you. You're only responsible for paying Lulu for the print costs and shipping. That's it!

## OTHER NOTABLE LULU FEATURES

This company is constantly expanding and improving upon what they offer for indie authors and hobbyists. Do you want to make a photo book, comic book, magazine, yearbook, or calendar? Then Lulu has what you need. What about a coil bound notebook that can serve as a companion journal for your latest underwater basketweaving book? Lulu has you covered.

Something I didn't discuss earlier was the free Lulu cover tool. I recommend a professional cover designer, but I know it's not affordable for everyone. The free cover tool might be your solution if you're working on a limited budget. Unfortunately, I have no experience using this tool, so I can't speak about its functionality and options.

Lulu continues to be an invaluable resource in the indie author community as they post informative videos on YouTube as part of Lulu University, which are hosted by Chelsea Bennett. And if you subscribe to their newsletter, you'll get notifications about free webinars with top experts, deals, discounts, and flash sales. Stay subscribed if you plan to use Lulu; the deals they share sometimes make up for the higher base costs.

# AGGREGATE PUBLISHER FOR AUDIOBOOKS #1: FINDAWAY VOICES BY SPOTIFY

**WEBSITE:** HTTPS://FINDAWAYVOICES.COM/

**DISTRIBUTION:** 24SYMBOLS, ANYPLAY, APPLE, AUDIBLE/AMAZON, AUDIOBOOKS.COM, AUDIOBOOKSNOW, AUDIOBOOKSNZ, BAJALIBROS, BAM, BEEK, BINGEBOOKS, BOKUS PLAY, BOOKMATE, CHIRP, CLIQ, DOWNPOUR, ESTORIES, GOOGLE PLAY, HUMMINGBIRD, INSTAREAD, KOBO/WALMART, LEAMOS, LIBRO.FM, MILKBOX, NEXTORY, NOOK AUDIOBOOKS, SCRIBD, STORYTELLER, UBOOK, 3LEAF GROUP, AXIELL, BAKER & TAYLOR, BIBLIOTHECA, BIDI, EBSCO, FOLLETT, HOOPLA, MLOL, ODILO, OVERDRIVE, PERMA-BOUND, ULVERSCROFT, AND WHEELERS

---

Let's briefly pause from ebook and print book aggregators to focus on the audiobook aggregate publishing platform Findaway Voices by Spotify. Though we'll tackle other relevant options beyond audiobooks later, I felt it best to tackle Findaway Voices next because that's the third most used aggregate publisher on my publishing wide checklist. When I tackle wide audiobook publishing, my go-to avenues are ACX and Findaway Voices. You'll discover why when I break down the math.

Findaway Voices is a subsidiary of the Findaway company based out of Solon, Ohio. Established in 2015, Findaway Voices was the parent company's foray into downloadable audiobook content.

Previously, the Findaway company only managed physical audiobook distribution. The company did something right because in late 2021, Spotify acquired the company for audiobook distribution.

*Side note: Spotify's acquisition of Findaway Voices has had its share of criticism from authors, especially when they changed the Terms of Use in early 2024. Many authors viewed the change as a rights grab, and a mass exodus ensued. Thankfully, the public outcry was enough for Findaway Voices to course-correct immediately.*

In 2019, I visited the Findaway Voices Headquarters to tour their two large office buildings with hundreds of employees. Findaway Voices was customer-centered and author-centric. They didn't just want to see their authors happy; they wanted their partners happy with the quality of content they submitted for distribution. Findaway Voices ensures audiobook files meet specifications by notifying rights holders of issues and providing guidance for distribution.

To be very clear, Findaway Voices only distributes audiobooks, and it's better that way. You'll discover, if you haven't already, that publishing audiobooks can be time-consuming and not very cheap. Using an aggregate publisher that specializes in audio makes it simple to publish wide. Then, you won't have to ask yourself, "Did I remember to publish the audiobook and ebook on this platform?"

Yeah, I've been there far too many times and hope to guide you away from those issues.

Even though Findaway Voices didn't launch until 2015, they still have the widest reach of any audiobook publishing platform, including ACX. Currently, Findaway Voices distributes to over forty different retail and audiobook distributors, but that number fluctuates based on who they have agreements with and for how long. I only ever see them remove a distributor when the platform folds. Findaway Voices notifies its rights holders when they add or subtract any options.

Speaking of changes, in 2024, Spotify removed the marketplace where account holders and narrators could connect. This move wasn't well-received since quite a few authors relied on that marketplace to hire narrators or voice-over talent for their projects. This means if you want to publish through Findaway Voices, you must come with a completed audiobook.

The royalty structure can be slightly confusing, especially since Findaway Voices doesn't provide any public-facing pages with royalty amounts. Visit the Payment Terms link at the bottom of your dashboard for a detailed breakdown. The royalty rate fluctuates between 25% to 50%. Much like the previous self-publishing options, Findaway Voices takes a 20% cut from the net profit, leaving you with the remaining 80%.

Keep in mind, this doesn't account for pool subscription or cost-per-checkout models since you're paid from a pool of money based on performance. You can choose to work with those platforms or deselect them for distribution should you find the agreement unfavorable. Take your time looking through all your options to ensure it's a good fit. I recommend trying them out for a few months, then assess if you should keep your audiobook up or remove it from those distribution options.

Before you turn your nose up at them, consider the biggest advantage to using Findaway Voices: Spotify. You don't have to worry about any intermediary since Findaway Voices publishes to Spotify direct. With Spotify owning Findaway Voices, the revenue share is just 50%, with no additional platform fees. Over the past few years, Spotify has made it their mission to expand audiobook offerings aggressively, gearing themselves up to topple the dominant audiobook retailer, Audible. Competition is good, especially for authors, since now we have choices beyond just another Amazon-owned company.

Spotify must've been aware that ACX-exclusive authors get 100 promotional codes to distribute, so they followed suit. On ACX, you can only request 25 promo codes at a time and can't ask for more until you disperse what you have. Unlike Audible, Spotify provides its promo codes with each publication in your dashboard. Also, Spotify is available in far more regions than Audible, reaching even more audiobook listeners.

Findaway Voices pays royalties thirty days after the close of the month. For example, any sales made in January would show up in late February. They pay through direct deposit, wire transfer, or PayPal with a $10 minimum payment threshold.

# AGGREGATE PUBLISHER FOR AUDIOBOOKS #2: AUTHOR'S REPUBLIC

**WEBSITE:** AUTHORSREPUBLIC.COM

**DISTRIBUTION:** AUDIBLE/AMAZON, APPLE, AUDIOBOOK STORE, AUDIOTEKA, BEHEAR, BOOKBEAT, BOOKWALKER, DIVIBIB, EBSCO INFORMATION SERVICES, ESTORIES, FONOS, GLOBOOK, GRUPO VI-DA, HIBOOKS, KIDS.RADIO, LISTENERU, MACKIN, PERMABOUND, POCKETFM, RAHVA RAAMAT, SPEECHIFY, THE AUDIOBOOK STORE, YOUSCRIBE, LEAF GROUP, 24SYMBOLS, ANYPLAY, APPLE, AUDIOBOOKS NOW, AUDIOBOOKS.COM, BAKER & TAYLOR, INC., BEEK, BIBLIOTHECA, BOOKMATE, BOOKS-A-MILLION, CHIRP, CLIQ DIGITAL, DOWNPOUR, FOLLETT LIBRARY RESOURCES, GOOGLE, HOOPLA, INSTAREAD, KOBO, LIBRO.FM, MLOL, MY AUDIOBOOK LIBRARY, NEXTORY, NOOK, ODILO, OVERDRIVE, RADISH, EVERAND (FKA SCRIBD), SPOTIFY, STORYTEL, UBOOK, ULVERSCROFT, WHEELERS BOOK CLUB LIMITED, SPOTIFY STREAMING, DEEZER, NAPSTER, APPLE MUSIC, YOUTUBE MUSIC, AND CALM RADIO

Founded in 2015, Author's Republic is an audiobook distributor that reaches over fifty-seven platforms. Findaway Voices used to be the dominant force in wide audiobooks, but over the past several years, Author's Republic has stepped up to offer another alternative.

While Findaway Voices no longer has a marketplace for narrators and voice-over talent, Author's Republic picked up the slack when they launched their own marketplace. This is similar to Audiobook

Creation Exchange, where you can get your audiobook produced and published all in one spot, removing any friction you'd otherwise experience when searching for experienced professionals. The shocking part is the relatively inexpensive rates narrators charge compared to platforms like ACX or Findaway Voice's defunct marketplace.

Most narrators and voice-over talent charge a per-finished-hour (PFH) rate, based on the finished product rather than the production time. On average, it takes five to seven hours to produce one hour of content.[xv] For example, a three-hour audiobook could take anywhere from fifteen to twenty-one hours to produce.

Creating audiobooks requires time, expertise, and, sometimes, outside help, so producers will charge anywhere from $125 to $250 per finished hour as a minimum. That same three-hour audiobook can cost between $375 and $750. If you're an epic novelist or a prolific author, producing an audiobook can be quite the money pit.

In the marketplace for Author's Republic, you'll find quite a few narrators who charge as low as $45 to $60 per finished hour. That drives down production cost for the three-hour audiobook to $135 to $180, making it much more affordable. However, research these cheaper options before committing to anything. Lower costs don't always equate to higher value or quality.

When you're ready to work with a narrator, you'll submit payment to Author's Republic, who'll hold the deposit in escrow until the project completes.

Should you already have your audiobook production ready before getting to Author's Republic, you can still publish content through them. The specifications and requirements are nearly identical to ACX, so you won't find any surprises here.

Author's Republic offers three distinct distribution options:

1. Audible/Amazon
2. Retail and Library Channels = 51 options
3. Music Channels = 4 options

You can opt-in to any of the three options. Should you see a specific avenue you don't want to reach, you'll have to contact support to remove that option. For example, if your audiobook is already on Apple, you can contact support to remove it from distribution through Author's Republic.

In years past, I was reluctant to use Author's Republic because they had a similar stance to IngramSpark: all or nothing. Now, they're much more flexible. You'll want to cross-check the overlapping options between Author's Republic and Findaway Voices to avoid duplicate publishing.

> *Side note: One exception to this duplicate publishing rule is when publishing to Apple through ACX or Findaway Voices; Apple will always default to Findaway Voices because they're a preferred partner.*

Author's Republic may take up to sixty business days to distribute your audiobook to all retailers after publication. Check each site individually, and remember, you can opt in or out of various channels. If you don't see your audiobook on a particular channel, you may not have selected it for distribution there.

There are three different status options in your Author's Republic dashboard which allow you to know at a glance how close your audiobook is to going live on a specific platform. Here's what you might see:

1. Opted out: This means you selected this option because you did not want your audiobook sold via that channel.
2. In Distribution Queue: That literally means it's underway; Author's Republic is working on getting your audiobook distributed through their various partners. This can take some time and is essentially a "pending" status for that title.
3. Sent: Author's Republic has distributed your audiobook to the channel, and the status is out of their hands.

Links to your title will display below the retailer when it's available, but even though a link doesn't appear doesn't mean it's not there. Sometimes, you'll have to search to find your book on that retailer's website, which is no big deal.

> *Pro Tip: When you get your audiobook retail links, update your universal book links generated through Books2Read. Every bit of friction you remove brings your readers one step closer to buying and listening to your audiobook.*

Author's Republic takes 30% of net profits, leaving authors with the remaining 70%. Much like the previous aggregate publishing companies, Author's Republic has individual royalty agreements in place with their partners. It gets more complicated, as you'd guess, when you identify what each partner does: retail, subscription model, library model, and more.

Unfortunately, Author's Republic doesn't disclose the royalty agreement for each partner, leaving account holders in the dark. Contact support if you want a full breakdown of every avenue, each royalty, and the specific model.

The beautiful part about Author's Republic is, like Findaway Voices, you get to set your own audiobook price. By comparison, ACX determines the price of your audiobook based on the length. This rule applies to most audiobooks hitting the Amazon and Audible platforms. Expect a 30% decrease in royalties using Amazon and Audible versus ACX. Where you give up pricing control for a higher royalty through ACX, you're sacrificing royalty for pricing control through Author's Republic.

I recommend going direct to the source and deselecting Amazon/Audible in your Author's Direct account. The two exceptions to that advice are:

1. You don't want to bother with the extra account.
2. You're not able to set up an ACX account based on your region.

If you're unable to set up an ACX account but want the best royalty possible for Amazon and Audible, then go with Findaway Voices since they have an 80/20 revenue split on Amazon/Audible sales versus the 70/30 split that Author's Republic offers.

Author's Republic pays account holders through PayPal or direct deposit with a minimum payment threshold of $10. You'll get paid thirty days after the end of the month, but keep in mind that each retailer has a different payment schedule. Adjust accordingly.

The Alliance of Independent Author's Watchdog List lists Author's Republic as a partner with an excellent rating. The Watchdog list is a well-vetted catalogue of companies and services within the publishing industry, so you can expect this company to be trustworthy and reliable. You're in excellent hands.

# CHAPTER 4:
# MISCELLANEOUS AGGREGATE PUBLISHERS

The publishing options I've shared so far are the best and the brightest, in my experience. But there are a few more notable options worth considering based on your specific wants and needs.

The following options are companies I've investigated for my podcast but have yet to try them out. They all come with mostly positive reviews from authors. I'll briefly summarize each option and encourage you to visit The Alliance of Independent Authors' Watchdog List to cross-check any company or service.

## STREETLIB

Founded in 2006 and based in Italy, Streetlib is an aggregate publishing platform that offers wide distribution for ebooks, audiobooks, and, to a limited extent, paperback books. Unfortunately, print book distribution is only available to European account holders. But their array of ebook and audiobook distribution options are plentiful.

Streetlib currently provides a free plan for up to ten ebook titles with limited distribution and 70% of net royalties. The Pro subscription gives you access to all formats—ebook, print book, and audiobook—

with a limit of 100 titles for $99 per year. You'll earn an 85% royalty, plus reach over fifty retailers. Essentially, if you want to make the most of Streetlib, you'll have to upgrade to their Pro plan.

Streetlib's subscription plan is like what PublishDrive offers. I'm partial to PublishDrive only because I've been using their platform since 2018. However, I've had quite a few great conversations with Streetlib and have only heard good things about the platform.

The ALLi Watchdog list currently lists Streetlib as a partner with an excellent rating.

## BLURB

Founded in 2005, Blurb is a print-on-demand company that is a go-to source for publishing high-quality print books. Although Blurb offers many tools and services, they come at a high cost. The base cost for print books is astronomical compared to the other platforms. I ordered about four different proofs from Blurb and didn't find the quality that much better than the rest.

However, if you're an author looking for unique publishing options like photo books, magazines, or wall art, then Blurb might be for you. They offer distribution through Ingram Book Group, so that means they reach over 40,000 online retailers, libraries, and bookstores.

Should you plan to use Blurb, be prepared to charge your readers higher prices than normal in order to make any money per sale. While you might sell a print book for $19.99 through Amazon KDP, you'll have to charge somewhere north of $29.99 to see a similar profit.

The other unfortunate part of Blurb is they only offer three trim sizes: 5x8, 6x9, 8x10. You can print your book in paperback, hardcover, or hardcover with dust jacket. The royalty rate is 45% minus print fees with the comprehensive distribution option. For the much narrower option of broad distribution, the royalty rate is 60% minus print fees.

Blurb has an excellent rating with the ALLi Watchdog List, so they're verified as legit. You can proceed with caution, and I highly recommend ordering proofs from Blurb to compare to other companies for yourself. You might disagree with my take on the print quality, so give them a shot if you're interested.

## BOOKBABY

Founded in 2011, this full-service aggregate publishing site offers distribution for authors. BookBaby distributes ebooks, print books, and audiobooks. Account holders have to pay a substantial fee upfront, but they reap the rewards on the back end because they collect 100% of net profits.

Do you remember PublishDrive's subscription model? Well, BookBaby is similar except you pay for everything up front, not in recurring monthly installments. The biggest issue you'll encounter is that BookBaby charges a fee whenever you need to push updates or make minor corrections, whether reformatting a file or uploading the corrected version.

BookBaby handles everything from editing to interior formatting to cover design to marketing and beyond. I interviewed a couple of authors who gave high marks to BookBaby's service. Those authors agreed that BookBaby is pricey compared to other self-publishing companies, but the authors admitted to feeling less overwhelmed and more focused on other aspects of their life and business. Had they chosen other aggregate distributors, they would've had to handle all the editing, interior formatting, and cover design on their own. Having a deeper budget allowed them more time to focus on other things in their lives and businesses.

For ebook distribution with BookBaby, you'll pay $299 to reach over 170 countries and 60+ stores. That's *just* for the bare minimum distribution. Authors without a completed book will need to pay for services to handle any aspects they can't manage themselves. For instance, if you handle all the editing but not the cover design or interior formatting, you can have BookBaby complete those for you.

For print book distribution, you'll pay $399 for distribution to over fifty online retailers, libraries and bookstores. You'll never guess who fulfills some of their print distribution: Ingram Book Group. BookBaby appears to hit some avenues not covered by Ingram Book Group, so you may reach beyond the 40,000 options IngramSpark offers.

Should you not be interested in the widest distribution, you can always pay a lower fee of $149 for access to the BookBaby Bookshop where you'll receive a 50% royalty.

BookBaby doesn't offer distribution for audiobooks beyond their BookBaby Bookshop, which you must pay $99 to access. The great part though is you earn a 75% royalty, which is well above the average audiobook royalty rate of 40% to 50%. I foresee them expanding audiobook distribution at some point, but for now, you at least have an alternative to ACX, the low-ball platform.

## OTHER MISCELLANEOUS OPTIONS TO CONSIDER

Admittedly, I wish I could cover all options for self-publishing books wide, but for brevity's sake, I'm limiting it to what I know, like, trust, and have used. I've explored a range of self-publishing platforms and have a few still on my radar. Give these options a look:

1. **XinXii:** This German-based company offers tools and resources for publishing and distributing ebooks and audiobooks. Everything looks great on the surface, but account holders and authors have complained about the lack of customer support. The few authors who use XinXii claim it's actually a great platform. Proceed with caution.

2. **Tablo:** This company offers distribution for ebooks, print books, and audiobooks with a subscription model like PublishDrive.

3. **Audiobooks Unleashed:** This site originally started as a premium marketing resource for audiobooks but has recently expanded to include distribution. The catch? They vet every audiobook and author coming to their platform to make sure that what they publish can truly get a return on their investment. It's kind of like traditional publishing in that you have to impress the folks at Audiobooks Unleashed to gain access to distribution. Some authors complain of spotty customer support, but I've yet to experience issues with them responding. Take that with a grain of salt since I have a fairly public platform that comes with unimplied consequences of not answering.

4. **Lantern Audio:** Formerly known as ListenUp Audio, this

company is a full-service solution for audiobook distribution. I had the pleasure of speaking with a team member, and he was nothing short of helpful. Think of Lantern Audio as the audiobook equivalent to BookBaby but with wider reach.

5. **Spoken.Press:** This digital narration platform sets itself apart from the rest of the pack with their ethically sourced narrators and voice-over talent. They're still relatively new to the game, but from what I've seen so far, they could position themselves to be a worthy competitor to sites like Speechify or Google Play Books.

## A FRIENDLY REMINDER ABOUT PUBLISHING EVERYWHERE

If your goal is to be on every retail website and brick-and-mortar bookstore, by all means, try to hit all the options. On average, when I'm publishing wide, it'll take me about three hours to handle ebook, paperback, and hardcover. Now, imagine tacking on all these other miscellaneous options. It becomes a tall ask and a bit of a drag.

Wider doesn't always equal better payouts. Listing your book on some obscure retailer in Indonesia doesn't always equate to sales. Let's say you spend three hours or more publishing your content, then you discover a typo or need to update something. You'd have to revisit every site, wasting another three hours of your time. To make matters worse, when you build a deep backlog of books, you're going to have to update them at some point. Welp, there's another three hours there.

Can you imagine publishing over twelve books per year? You've officially got a full-time job managing all those publications across multiple accounts!

Be selective about how wide you go. If you're new to the game, I recommend starting with just one new option. Experiment with the platform, explore its tools, and mastermind with other authors about getting the most from that distribution. A great place to connect with your peers is in my Discord community ([DaleLinks.com/Discord](DaleLinks.com/Discord)).

# CHAPTER 5:
# SELF-DISTRIBUTION/DIRECT SALES

All self-published authors should consider direct sales, whether through their own websites or other digital storefronts. It allows your avid readers to support you directly. Some authors sell their ebooks and print books with a basic product page that has an image, a description, and a PayPal checkout button. While other authors rely on premium services to handle direct sales.

Start with what you can afford, then upgrade as your budget or time allows. You can make direct sales work for you with no recurring monthly subscription fees.

## DIRECT SALES FOR YOUR WEBSITE

Shopify is a premium e-commerce platform with a monthly subscription, while WooCommerce is a free plugin for WordPress. Both options, along with APIs (Application Programming Interfaces), integrate seamlessly with Bookvault and Lulu Direct to manage direct sales orders.

The e-commerce platform Payhip and the website-building platform Wix integrate with Bookvault, providing even more flexibility for sellers. Best of all, neither Bookvault nor Lulu Direct takes a cut of your earnings; they only charge for printing and shipping costs. Beyond that, all royalties are yours to keep.

Be prepared to explore and experiment with Bookvault and Lulu before you launch the book to the public. Each platform comes with a steep learning curve, and they even encourage account holders to run test orders before sharing your book's product page.

I ran into an issue with Bookvault fulfilling a print order through a sale in Payhip. Thankfully, support got back to me within a day, and I discovered I missed an option to enable my book for shipping. I would've known that had I read the free guide they provide.

## DIRECT SALES WITHOUT WEB HOSTING OR TECH SKILLS

If you're less enthusiastic about managing website sales and prefer a more hands-off approach, consider options that require less technical expertise.

In early 2024, IngramSpark launched their Share & Sell program, where you can create a direct sales landing page for a book. You can make the link public or keep it private, generate promotional codes, and even limit the number of books sold. Would you like to do a flash sale for your loyal readers or email subscribers? Then Share & Sell is for you.

To set it up, you just follow a few prompts, then you'll be done. It literally takes less than five minutes to create a page. You'll get a link and QR code you can share everywhere. The one issue is the program is only available in the US, but they're looking to expand to the UK, Canada, Australia, and beyond. As previously mentioned, there's a $3.50 surcharge per sale. Compare that to Lulu Direct or Bookvault, which do not charge additional fees.

The digital ecommerce platforms Gumroad and Payhip are two excellent places to sell your digital and, to a limited extent, your physical goods.

## DIRECT SALES WITH GUMROAD

Gumroad is an online platform with a user-friendly interface that allows you to sell various types of digital content, including ebooks, music, software, courses, and more. The marketplace for Gumroad gets steady online traffic; I've seen plenty of organic sales on products despite my lack of effort to market them. They accept and dispense payments through PayPal. Account holders can expect to get payment every Friday after the close of a week.

You can sell your ebooks and set up a checkout for print orders, but it'll be entirely up to you to get a print copy and ship it to the customer. Is self-fulfillment of print purchases ideal? No, but it's a practical solution for anyone who doesn't want to fuss with ecommerce tools like Shopify.

You'll want to upload all iterations of your ebook, but if you want Gumroad to supply a digital watermark on all copies sold, provide the PDF version.

The royalty you'll earn is 90% minus payment processing fees, which is usually around 2.9% plus a $0.49 transaction fee. If you're not digging the royalty or the transaction fee, then you'll want to look into Payhip.

## DIRECT SALES WITH PAYHIP

Payhip offers everything Gumroad does and more. This includes the clean user-interface, digital marketplace, and dead simple process for publishing. The two advantages Payhip has over Gumroad are the royalty rate and print-on-demand integration with Bookvault.

With Payhip's free plan, you'll pay a 5% transaction fee per sale, plus payment processing fees (via PayPal or Stripe). The $29 per month plan lowers the transaction fee to 2%, while payment processing fees stay the same. The top-tier plan at $99 per month drops transaction fees entirely, leaving only the payment processing fees.

Much like Gumroad, you can upload a PDF for your ebook, and they'll give each customer a unique digital watermark to prevent piracy.

The biggest advantage Payhip has over Gumroad is the direct integration with Bookvault. Setting it up is a little confusing at first, but if you read the guide Bookvault provides, you should have it all set up in less than five minutes.

But what if you need something simpler than Payhip and Gumroad for distributing ebooks or want a better royalty? Let's talk about the latest player in the self-publishing game: Laterpress.

## DIRECT SALES FOR EBOOKS WITH LATERPRESS

Founded in 2022, Laterpress is a digital publishing platform for authors to sell ebooks direct to their customers for a 100% royalty minus payment processing fees through Stripe. You keep all the profits from any sales you make. When Laterpress recommends a sale, they take a 10% cut. When an author sends a customer, they get 5% per sale. This means you can make anywhere from an 85% to 100% royalty per sale.

The Laterpress platform operates under the control of its user base, with account holders driving changes and additions. You won't find this business model with platforms like KDP.

Because the user base requested direct sales for audiobooks, they're right now in closed beta for access with plans to roll out full access to everyone going into 2025 and beyond. I'm sure by the time this book hits press, they'll be in open beta and ready for the public to test it out. Admittedly, I have high hopes but realistic expectations. This new feature will take some time to iterate and improve, so growing pains and mistakes will happen.

Should you ever have any issues or problems, the Laterpress support team is eagerly standing by to help. Their Discord community is another great place to learn about upcoming features, get questions answered, and interact with other authors leveraging their platform.

I see big things on the horizon for this relative newcomer in the self-publishing space. Check it out for yourself and see what you think.

## PREMIUM SERVICES FOR BOOK MARKETING & DIRECT SALES

StoryOrigin is the book marketing tool for indie authors that's the equivalent of a Swiss Army Knife. You can collaborate with authors in newsletter swaps and group promos, build an advance reader copy team, gather beta reader notes, distribute audiobook promo codes, and more. Their monthly plan runs about $8 to $10 per month to give you all features, including direct sales for ebooks.

All you have to do is provide StoryOrigin with the metadata and interior content, then you'll have a professional product page in minutes. The best part? You only have to sweat payment processing fees through LemonSqueezy (5% plus $0.30 transaction fee). This comes in just below what Payhip offers and is significantly better than Gumroad.

The only catch is you have to pay monthly dues for StoryOrigin. Fortunately, they have more features beyond direct sales, so this tool will serve many uses in your author business.

I've heard many great things about BookFunnel, a service similar to StoryOrigin. You can set up direct sales for ebooks and audiobooks through BookFunnel for roughly the same price as StoryOrigin.

Between the two services, I'll recommend StoryOrigin only because I've known and used that tool since 2020. BookFunnel is something I've only recently discovered. You can't go wrong with either company, so give them a look if you want more tools from a single platform than just a direct sales option.

# CHAPTER 6:
# WHERE TO START

In the following chapters, I'll break down my approach to wide publishing based on no upfront investment while getting the best possible royalty. For instance, you could publish your ebook to Apple through various avenues, but you'll get the most ideal payout publishing direct through Apple Books for Authors. Or, if you want to distribute your book through OverDrive, then you'll want to use Kobo Writing Life to get the highest payout possible. This eliminates a few options and also comes with some restrictions (i.e., update fees). If you see one avenue that is inaccessible or unappealing to you, simply remove it from the list. Refer to the miscellaneous options for wide publishing to fill in the gaps, but be prepared to either pay money upfront or lose some distribution options you'd otherwise get through my suggestions.

You can follow along by completing the three-step process, but you must have your book ready to go (i.e., edited and formatted). The first step is setting up the accounts. You'll need to provide each platform with relevant payment and tax information before you can continue to the subsequent steps. All platforms require this regardless of tax laws. If you get stuck, contact customer support from the platform.

The platforms I chose may make changes, so double-check each avenue for all their partners and terms of use when you're ready to start. I can't guarantee that what I share in this book will stay accurate for years to come. You'll know for sure whether a distribution partner is or isn't available when you go to publish your book. Worst-case scenario: You just stop short of publishing the book should you find an avenue is missing that you wanted.

The second step in the three-step process is to get your book project in order. This includes:

1. Your metadata
2. Your cover, interior, and audio files
3. Optional: ISBN

To make life a little easier for you, I whipped together a metadata template that you can use for all your projects. The sheet includes all relevant information like the title, subtitle, author name, description, keywords, and more. Visit DaleLinks.com/MetadataSheet to download a free copy. This sheet will be a lifesaver, especially when you're marketing and promoting your book. Instead of typing everything a thousand times, type it once and then copy and paste the content wherever you need it later.

I have a very specific reason for the steps I follow when I publish a book, but if you feel like deviating from that path, go for it. The rare exception to the rule is when you're publishing print books via KDP and IngramSpark. Since both platforms distribute to Amazon, some issues might crop up. You might get a notification that the "ISBN is already in use." To avoid that, you'll want to publish your book on KDP and IngramSpark back-to-back. I've never had issues and have published dozens of books this way. Does it have to be a perfectly sequenced book upload and publishing? No, but that certainly won't hurt.

My preference is to tackle the iterations in this order:

1. Ebook
2. Print books
3. Audiobook

Then, I publish to the platforms I prefer most to least. Switch that as you see fit. Again, just avoid duplicate publishing to any one retail platform.

When you come to an avenue that's inaccessible or that you don't prefer, browse the list of aggregate publishing platforms. For example, should you find Draft2Digital doesn't have what you want and Streetlib does, give Streetlib a shot. Self-publishing isn't paint-by-numbers, so tweak my plan to suit your needs. Whatever paths you choose, be sure to write them down so you don't forget for future updates and new publications.

Any author planning a book launch should give themselves plenty of runway before the official launch. Most platforms have a pre-order or scheduling feature to remove any friction or stress that goes into launching a book on a set date. If a hard launch date isn't a big deal, fire when ready.

The one avenue you'll want to give yourself more room for distribution is ACX. They currently do not have a pre-order or scheduled release feature. The real pain in the neck is that they assure authors it takes up to ten business days for them to approve a title for release, but it's been my experience that can take upwards of two months before the audiobook is available for purchase on the site.

Findaway Voices and Author's Republic have much faster processing times, but you'll still want to give yourself about a month or so before your official book launch. It takes a while for them to distribute your book and for the partners to publish it on their respective platforms.

If you're ever lost, contact Support on the platform you need help with. And join my Discord community, where there are over 1,000 active members. We've got an amazing crop of authors and self-publishers who come with various experience levels and insights. Heck, you might even learn something new that you wouldn't have otherwise picked up from me. Visit [DaleLinks.com/Discord](DaleLinks.com/Discord) and make sure you let me know when you arrive by tagging my name (@selfpubwithdale).

Now, let's publish your books wide!

# CHAPTER 7:
# WIDE PUBLISHING FOR EBOOKS

## STEP 1: ONE-TIME SET UP

Set up all your accounts with an email you access daily. This email address is your lifeline; do NOT take it for granted. Keep it organized so you know when a publishing company needs something from you or has to communicate something important. KDP is notorious for emailing account holders and giving them a three-day window to respond. When authors don't respond, KDP swiftly terminates the account.

Err on the side of caution and use a legitimate email that you check daily.

Open accounts at:

- Amazon Kindle Direct Publishing (KDP)
- Apple Books for Authors
- Barnes & Noble Press: Set up this account ASAP because they take a while to approve new accounts. Their vetting process is slow, and many authors have complained over

the years about the delays.
- Kobo Writing Life (KWL)
- Draft2Digital (D2D): If you plan to use D2D for distributing to the previous four options, you can disregard setting up those other accounts.
- Google Play Books Partner Center (GPBPC)
- Lulu
- Payhip
- Laterpress
- OPTIONAL—PublishDrive: I know I'm pushing my luck here since PublishDrive technically has a monthly subscription fee, but they have the free plan for one ebook. Take advantage of that freebie.
- OPTIONAL—Gumroad: Even though I'm a huge fan of Gumroad, I prefer Payhip because of its better royalty rate and sleek user interface. Selecting this avenue will provide you with access to Gumroad's Marketplace, where you'll get tons of organic traffic.

## STEP 2: PREPARATION

Store all of the contents in a project folder named after the book's title. In the event you have many iterations of your manuscript, create an ARCHIVE folder within your main project folder. Dump all inessential elements for publishing in the ARCHIVE folder. Yes, I put that in all caps because that's attention grabbing and you'll make no mistake about what's in that folder. I break up content into separate subfolders based on their purposes.

I'll add folders for promotional materials and platform-specific subfolders to simplify uploads. For instance, I have a folder specifically for Payhip and StoryOrigin, since they have different requirements than the self-publishing platforms.

Get your metadata ready by filling out all relevant information on the metadata sheet (DaleLinks.com/MetadataSheet). Then, when you visit each site, just copy and paste what you have prepared. I save myself a *lot* of time with this metadata template, so do yourself a favor and create one for every book you have.

Place the metadata sheet in the main project folder so it's readily accessible. Within that main project folder, create a sub-folder for your cover files and a sub-folder for your interiors. I recommend having your ebook in the following formats:

- epub
- PDF
- mobi

Even though Amazon is phasing out the mobi file, it's still a good idea to keep it on hand as some platforms and readers still use it. Epub is the gold standard for ebook file types. PDF works well for those who don't use an ereader or ereading app and prefer reading on larger devices.

You don't need all those files, but you will certainly limit yourself since some platforms require those files. I have Miblart, my cover design service, create the epub and PDF formats. Then, I convert the epub into a mobi file using the free open source software, Calibre.

Here's how to convert an epub into a mobi file using Calibre:

1. Click "Add books" in the top right corner of the Calibre dashboard.
2. Upload your epub file.
3. Then, select "Convert books" from the top menu. A pop-up will appear with your book.
4. In the top right dropdown menu next to "Output format," select mobi.
5. Click OK, then wait about a minute.
6. You'll see the Folder option on the right below your book's details. Click the Book file's hyperlink to access your formatted interior.
7. Grab the mobi file and move it to the folder with your interiors.

I recommend you label your files with the title, file type, and date. It's easy for quick access and snap decisions. As an example, I'd label the files for this book on December 6, 2024, like this:

- Wide Publishing for Authors - epub 120624
- Wide Publishing for Authors - mobi 120624
- Wide Publishing for Authors - PDF 120624

I put all the interiors into one folder for both ebook and print, as the PDF typically works for print. That's another reason I hire professionals for interior formatting—I avoid wasting time figuring out the best way to format it for print.

Next, create another subfolder in the main project folder for your cover design. You can use this folder for all iterations, just make sure you use the same label as the ebook interiors. If you really want to be fastidious, place a number in front of the label for each file which signifies the order of importance in the upload process. You can then organize that folder alphabetically and easily find the files you need based on the publishing process you're handling.

Save your cover design files to that folder. You'll need the .jpg file for pretty much every platform. Will some websites accept other file types? Yes, but most every self-publishing platform accepts .jpg, so you might as well keep your folders clutter free and run with one file type per publication type.

## STEP 3: HIT THE CHECKLIST

Open up your book's metadata sheet and minimize it on your screen. Then, you'll open up your internet browser. For any avenue you plan to use, bookmark and file the hyperlinks in a folder on your browser. When you visit these sites later, you can open all links at one time when you right-click the bookmarks folder and select "Open All in New Window." Boom! Time saved for future visits.

Remember, even if you're not planning to publish more than one book wide, you still will have to update your book, so you'll need a quick path to open those websites in separate browser tabs.

If you don't follow an assembly line process, you can miss the finer details on each platform. Give your undivided attention to each website when you're uploading so you don't miss any details or upload the wrong file because you're too busy trying to be efficient.

Yes. That's happened to me…multiple times.

In my list below, you'll see I go direct to the four Amazon alternatives. If you'd rather not go through the extra work and are okay sacrificing 10% of retail price per sale of your ebook, use Draft2Digital. D2D manages distribution for Apple, Kobo Writing Life, Kobo Plus, OverDrive, and Barnes & Noble.

# THE WIDE PUBLISHING CHECKLIST FOR EBOOKS

- ☐ Amazon KDP: Do *not* opt your ebook into KDP Select Program. You'll see this choice on the third step of the upload process.
- ☐ Apple Books for Authors
- ☐ Barnes & Noble Press
- ☐ Kobo Writing Life: Enable your ebook for Kobo Plus across all regions and give permission to be included in any new regions they roll out in the future. Next, opt into OverDrive and set your pricing. The general recommendation is setting the cost at two to three times the retail value.
- ☐ Draft2Digital: If you used any of the previous options, deselect them in the last step in the publishing process. This includes Apple, Kobo Writing Life, Kobo Plus, OverDrive, Barnes & Noble Press, and Amazon.
- ☐ Google Play Books Partner Center
- ☐ Lulu: I strictly use the Lulu Bookstore and avoid global distribution since that's covered through the previous avenues. Also, you avoid the $4.99 ebook fee for global distribution.

- [ ] Payhip: You can provide the PDF and even have Payhip place a watermark over it. If you're not concerned about pirates, you can always zip all three iterations of the ebook into a file with a set of directions on how to access your book on an ereader. The easiest solution is sending readers to Amazon's Send to Kindle page at Amazon.com/SendToKindle.

- [ ] Laterpress: Be prepared to spend some extra time to work on formatting. To get started, you can import your documents, but you'll have to fiddle with the formatting before hitting the publish button.

- [ ] OPTIONAL—PublishDrive: Deselect all previously published options and be mindful of overlapping with Draft2Digital. You could technically lean in favor of PublishDrive to get higher royalties. But remember, you only get one free ebook to publish on PublishDrive so make it count. D2D gives you everything free for a cut of your revenue, no catch.

    - [ ] Deselect these overlapping avenues in one of your accounts, D2D or PublishDrive: Amazon, Apple, Barnes & Noble, Kobo, Kobo Plus, OverDrive, Tolino, Gardners, Everand, cloudLibrary, Baker & Taylor, Hoopla.

- [ ] OPTIONAL: Gumroad

Platforms like Payhip and Lulu will approve and publish your ebook right away. For other platforms, you can expect the publishing process to take anywhere from one to five days. Some partners are a bit slow through D2D, but that's nothing the aggregate publisher can change.

Keep an eye on your email inbox for notifications from these companies. However, not all of them, like GPBPC, Lulu, and Payhip, will notify you when your book goes live.

Once per week for about six to eight weeks after a publication, I'll update my universal book link through Draft2Digital's free universal book link service, Books2Read (B2R). You'll find the links you need for each platform in your dashboard, but occasionally, you might have to search each retail platform to get your links. B2R is decent at finding some of your ebook listings online. I'll check once per week for availability of all iterations across every major platform. Usually I have all avenues accounted for within the first month and a half since some retailers take longer than others to publish my product on their sites.

# CHAPTER 8:
# WIDE PUBLISHING FOR PRINT BOOKS

## STEP 1: ONE-TIME SET UP

Similar to the instructions for wide publishing ebooks, you'll need to open accounts with a valid email that you check regularly. If you already have access to Amazon KDP or Payhip from the previous checklist, then you're all set with them.

Do **NOT** set up multiple KDP accounts, because Amazon will terminate all business with you. Having more than one KDP account violates their Terms & Conditions. Speaking of setting up accounts, it's a good idea to review all terms and conditions for each platform. If you ever get lost, consult an attorney or Customer Support.

Open an account at:

- o Amazon Kindle Direct Publishing
- o IngramSpark
    - o An IngramSpark alternative
        - o Draft2Digital: If you're not a fan of IngramSpark or are currently using D2D for ebook distribution, this

can replace IngramSpark. It comes at the lower end of royalties, but you're not having to sweat update fees as much as IngramSpark.
- Bookvault
- Payhip
- Optional Sites:
  - Lulu: I only use Lulu is for their bookstore. Eventually, I may tap into Lulu Direct for direct sales.
  - Blurb: Similar to Lulu, the Blurb Bookstore is another avenue for exposure. Admittedly, I've yet to try them out, so proceed with caution.

## STEP 2: PREPARATION

Much like I mentioned in the previous checklist, organize all your files into a designated project folder with subfolders. Sorting your files will make a world of a difference when you're uploading and publishing your book. I rarely separate ebook and print book files; instead, I'll divide the interior and cover files into subfolders. You'll learn in the next checklist why I keep audiobook files in a separate folder from the rest.

By now, you should have your book's metadata sheet filled out (DaleLinks.com/MetadataSheet) with all the pertinent information. Be sure to put your word count and page count on the sheet, because you'll need that for some platforms and possibly for promotional campaigns which require either a page or word count, sometimes both.

You only need one metadata sheet for all iterations of your book. Keep it in the project folder for easy access. Having it readily available will streamline your upload process, allowing you to quickly copy and paste the details into each website.

The items you'll need for upload include:

1. Interior file PDF: You can use this file for both the paperback and hardcover editions as long as the sizes are the same. Avoid using other file types, since they are often less reliable than PDFs.
2. Cover file PDF: Your paperback and hardcover cover files will have different sizes, so prepare both files when you're ready to publish your book. The cover and interior files should remain separate.

Speaking of the cover file, when you create a print book cover, include your barcode with pricing information on the back. Having a barcode with the retail pricing on it makes it more marketable for brick-and-mortar bookstores. Store owners are less likely to stock a book if there's no clear pricing on the book; it creates more work for them on an already unproven author.

Having your own ISBN also increases the likelihood of brick-and-mortar stores stocking your book, among other factors. An International Standard Book Number is a universal identifier, which allows retailers and libraries to search for information about the book and to find its metadata.

Some sites offer free ISBNs, but you can only use the free number on the platform that provided it. You can't keep or transfer any free ISBN provided by a platform. It's like being invited to cook lunch at my place: You can bring your own cookware or use mine. When you leave, you can take your stuff with you—just leave my pots and pans.

Authors can buy ISBNs for their books through various regional registration organizations. You can find a full list of sites when you visit the International ISBN Agency online. The agency provides all pertinent information, including the website, contact information, and more.

You will need an ISBN for each iteration of your book: ebook, paperback, hardcover, and audiobook. Ebook and audiobook ISBNs aren't mandatory, as some sites use their own systems for identification (e.g., Amazon Standard Identification Number). However, I highly recommend wide-published authors get individual ISBNs for each book iteration, so it's easier to track sales globally and have fewer instances of redundant published books.

Once you have an ISBN for your book, you can generate a barcode for free using the Kindlepreneur's Free Barcode Generator ([DaleLinks.com/Barcode](DaleLinks.com/Barcode)). Enter your book's ISBN and retail cost, then you can download the image files for that. Slap it on your back cover in the proper spot, then you're good to go.

I usually create the barcodes for my cover designer, so all they have to do is put them on, and we're good. If you're creating your own design, simply drag and drop the barcode onto the book cover.

Remember, not all platforms have the same requirements for publishing, so you may have to adjust your interior and cover files to accommodate them. For instance, KDP's files will work for Bookvault, Payhip, and to a limited extent, IngramSpark and Lulu. However, the KDP files will most likely clash with Blurb, since they have completely different requirements.

Explore every platform before you officially launch your book. I like to create test uploads so I can play around with the features and see what I'm dealing with. I don't publish this test book; I use it to explore the features and familiarize myself with the process before publishing my actual work.

For instance, I discovered the interior files for KDP worked well for Lulu, but the cover design needed a slight modification to fit Lulu's standards. I simply tossed the PDF into GIMP (graphic design software), then stretched the image to fit the specs. The measurements were slightly larger, but not enough to make the cover look disproportionate. If you're working with a cover designer, you can always ask them to create a Lulu-specific cover. For instance, I always ask for KDP and IngramSpark iterations. Lulu is so easy to fix that I can't see having my designer waste their time or spend money that I don't have to.

One last note: Keep your retail cost the same across the board—this includes ebook and audiobook (the exception being ACX since they select the price). Within the metadata sheet, you can add pricing for the various regions. Keep track of those as you use each platform. You don't want to send mixed signals to distributors and retailers, so keep your retail cost the same for each iteration.

If you're unsure how to price your book, check out the bestsellers in your genre. They provide valuable insights into what customers are willing to pay. You don't need to match their prices exactly, but staying within a similar range can help meet reader expectations.

## STEP 3: HIT THE CHECKLIST

Efficiency is essential to avoid spending too much time uploading your files. Print book publishing can take longer because the files are larger compared to ebooks. Plan to set aside at least one to two hours to complete the process, especially if you're publishing both paperback and hardcover formats.

Save all the websites you'll need as bookmarks and organize them in a single folder in your browser. When you want to open all the publishing sites, right-click on the folder, then select "Open all in new window." Then you can easily go from one site to the next. Rearrange the icons in the order that you want to visit the sites.

# THE WIDE PUBLISHING CHECKLIST FOR PRINT BOOKS

**OPEN YOUR BOOK'S METADATA SHEET AND THE FOLLOWING WEBSITES:**

- ☐ Amazon Kindle Direct Publishing: Once you upload and publish your ebook here, most of the metadata will carry over to the print iterations. You'll just need to adjust the categories and pricing. **Avoid selecting the Expanded Distribution option for your paperback books.** We'll be covering the same distribution in the next platform upload in this list. You don't have to worry about that with the hardcover books now, but I'm sure Expanded Distribution will eventually be a possibility for both print books.

- ☐ IngramSpark
  - ☐ IngramSpark alternative, Draft2Digital: If you prefer not to use IngramSpark or are already using D2D for ebook distribution, D2D can be a great alternative. While it offers slightly lower royalties, it has the advantage of fewer update fees, making it a more cost-effective option.

- ☐ Bookvault: The user interface is unlike any of the other companies, so be prepared for a steep learning curve. Take your time exploring your dashboard. When in doubt, contact support for assistance. To get your first three upload fees waived, use coupon code BVDALE. Should you run out of those codes, become a member of ALLi. Bookvault waives all upload fees for members.

- ☐ Payhip: You have two options for fulfilling print orders: self-fulfilled or Bookvault-fulfilled. Bookvault offers a downloadable guide on how to synchronize your Payhip account. Read the entire manual, because you'll need to know what to do when you get a sale. Payhip will be the fastest and easiest to set up. I highly recommend generating additional images or graphics to include on your book's product page. Browsing customers can then see all that on an image carousel.
- ☐ OPTIONAL—Lulu: I primarily use Lulu for their bookstore and may eventually explore Lulu Direct. Since Ingram Book Group manages Lulu's global distribution, it serves as a print-on-demand alternative to IngramSpark or Draft2Digital.
- ☐ OPTIONAL—Blurb: Similar to Lulu, the Blurb Bookstore is another avenue of exposure. Admittedly, I've yet to break ground here, so lower your expectations if you're expecting thousands of organic sales here. Just like Lulu, Ingram Book Group handles Blurb's Global Retail Network, so this is yet another alternative to IngramSpark, D2D, and Lulu.

Take your time going through this checklist; upload times will vary from one retailer to the next. If you're feeling extra ambitious and don't want to wait on a file to upload and process, you can always move onto the next platform. Just be careful and don't lose your place. I prefer to wait it out so I don't miss anything in the publishing process for each website.

In case you haven't been keeping tabs, Ingram Book Group manages a lot of print distribution for companies like IngramSpark, Draft2Digital, Lulu, and Blurb. You'll get the best royalty with IngramSpark with Draft2Digital coming in second. However, you'll lose a significant cut when using Lulu and Blurb for print distribution. I recommend exploring all four options and ordering a proof from each to see what makes the most sense for you. If you can't swing proof copies, then select between IngramSpark and Draft2Digital.

Draft2Digital allows one free update every ninety days and charges $25 per update outside of that. IngramSpark allows unlimited updates in the first sixty days after publishing, but charges $25 per update thereafter. Yes, you can find codes for IngramSpark, but they've been harder to find over the last couple of years. If you're a member of ALLi, right now you get one free update per month.

If this list seems to be a bit much, scale it back to just KDP and IngramSpark or Draft2Digital. The only issue with D2D is that they do not publish hardcover yet. I'm sure D2D will have hardcover books at some point, but in the meantime, you'll have to rely on KDP and IngramSpark.

# CHAPTER 9:
# WIDE PUBLISHING FOR AUDIOBOOKS

## STEP 1: ONE-TIME SET UP

Keeping in line with the previous checklists, open each account with a valid email address. Bookmark the websites and organize them in one browser folder. The next time you visit the sites, you can right click on the folder, then select "Open all in new window."

Open accounts at:

- Audiobook Creation Exchange (ACX): If you're not in the US, UK, Canada, or Ireland, skip this website. They strictly prohibit accounts from outside these regions. No worries, though—Findaway Voices by Spotify and Author's Republic can still distribute your work to Amazon and Audible.
- Kobo Writing Life: You'll need to contact support to request access to publishing audiobooks. You will receive an email notification once it becomes available.
- Google Play Books Partner Center

- Findaway Voices by Spotify
  - Findaway Voices Alternative: Author's Republic—Much like Findaway Voices, you'll need to avoid Amazon/Audible, Google Play Books, Kobo, and Overdrive.
- OPTIONAL: Payhip and Gumroad

## STEP 2: PREPARATION

Remember how I had you sort your book into a main project folder, but then asked you to keep audiobooks separate? Digital audiobooks require more files and eat up more data on your hard drive. I recommend you put your cover in the same folder as the other cover iterations (ebook and print) but separate the audio files into one folder.

Label all your files according to the chapter title or heading, but precede it with a number that represents the order it appears. For instance, I'll label audio files like this:

- 1 Opening Credits
- 2 Introduction
- 3 Chapter 1 - Exclusive Distribution vs. Wide Distribution

This naming convention helps keep all files neatly organized, making the upload process dead simple. You'll never have a doubt about what gets uploaded. I tried publishing without these naming conventions and discovered real quick that it's a headache having to audit every audio file according to the manuscript to make sure I uploaded in the right order.

Do not forget to include a three- to five-minute sample of your audiobook, and place that at the end of your list or at the front of it preceded by 0. Every major audiobook publishing platform requires a sample, so have that ready to go before publishing.

Feel free to use that audio sample everywhere you wish because there's no exclusivity agreement barring you from sharing it through your website, social media, or places like YouTube.

For precise specifications for audiobooks, I highly recommend having your files adhere to Audiobook Creation Exchange's guidelines. They have the strictest specs of all audiobook publishing platforms, so if you nail it with them, you'll be good everywhere else.

When you have all your files in order, it's time to fill out the... say it with me...METADATA SHEET! I know it's repetitive, but it's worth saying again. I've seen authors struggle with minor issues in their business, wondering why they're getting nowhere. Minimize these distractions and repetitive tasks by tracking all your metadata on one sheet.

When you upload your audiobook, you'll have a metadata sheet readily available to copy and paste the content easily.

Much like publishing print books, this process can be time consuming. I do not recommend uploading to more than one platform at a time because it can get real messy real quick if you're not super careful.

Play it safe and publish to each website one at a time, starting a new upload only after completing the previous one.

## STEP 3: HIT THE CHECKLIST

Access all dashboards to the companies where you have accounts. You know the neat little trick I shared earlier, so open all windows from the bookmarks folder for audiobook publishing companies. Now it's time to get to work.

# THE WIDE PUBLISHING CHECKLIST FOR AUDIOBOOKS

- ☐ Audiobook Creation Exchange (ACX): Since you're publishing wide, you must choose non-exclusive. Ignore the option for Apple; Findaway Voices will be the de facto distributor since they're a preferred Apple partner.
- ☐ Kobo Writing Life: Once you request and get access, your audiobook can publish to Kobo, Kobo Plus, and OverDrive.
- ☐ Google Play Books Partner Center: You can upload your own audio files or use the GPBPC dashboard to generate digital narration. While the quality isn't perfect, it's a budget-friendly choice for those with limited resources.
- ☐ Findaway Voices by Spotify
    - ☐ Deselect any of the previously used options:
        - ☐ Amazon/Audible
        - ☐ Google Play Books
        - ☐ Kobo, Kobo Plus, and Overdrive
    - ☐ Author's Republic
        - ☐ If you plan to use both Findaway Voices and Author's Republic, remove these overlapping avenues in one of your accounts: 24Symbols,

3 Leaf Group, Anyplay, Apple, Audiobooks Now, Audiobooks.com, Baker & Taylor, Beek, Barnes & Noble (also known as Nook or Nook Audiobooks), Bibliotheca (also known as cloudLibrary), Bookmate, Books-A-Million, Chirp, Cliq, Downpour, Everand, Follett (also known as Follett Library Resources), Hoopla, Instaread, Libro.FM, Nextory, Odilo, Radish, Spotify, Storytel, Ubook, Ulverscroft, Wheelers (also known as Wheelers Book Club Limited).

- [ ] Optional: Payhip and Gumroad

Just a friendly reminder: Author's Republic recommends using either Findaway Voices by Spotify or Author's Republic, but there's no rule against using both. Just be mindful that you do *not* publish in the same avenues through both accounts. Again, retailers dislike redundant listings.

I foresee audiobook publishing to continue to improve and grow at a much faster pace than its counterparts now that digital narration (AI-created audio) is coming to the forefront. Platforms like Speechify, ElevenLabs, and Spoken.Press are disrupting the audiobook publishing industry and offering alternatives to the higher-priced narrators and voice-over talent. But I don't see it entirely replacing human-voiced content. There will always be a place in the market for old-fashioned human performance.

# CHAPTER 10:
# DO YOUR RESEARCH

Although I've made every effort to provide you with the most accurate information about publishing wide, the reality is that this business is constantly changing and evolving. Double-check all distribution channels you want to use before publishing. Avoid publishing the same book to a single retail platform because retailers don't like redundant product listings. If you're using the same ISBN for a book—whether ebook, print book or audiobook—you'll most likely get a notification that the ISBN is already in use. In that case, your distribution is probably overlapping.

Notifications alone won't prevent accidentally publishing your book to the same platform twice. The reality is you can literally publish the same book across multiple platforms in minutes, making it impossible for one platform to know the other is publishing your book twice to the same platform. An exception to the rule is when you publish through KDP and IngramSpark at the same time. This is perfectly acceptable; neither company objects. You'll end up with one product page.

I've shared several points for you to consider, but there may still be some gray areas or unexplored topics to address before you dive into wide publishing. The rest of this chapter covers frequently asked questions and considerations to help you decide what options might work best for your needs.

## RESEARCH COMPANY REPUTATION

Over the past several years, it's been my job to research and report the comings and goings of self-publishing companies like KDP, Draft2Digital, and more. But the problem with getting your intel from any one YouTuber is you might get a biased viewpoint. Or the YouTuber may miss vital details that could make a difference in your decision-making process.

Research and explore all the previously mentioned options. You can crosscheck any of the sites I mentioned through the ALLi Watchdog List or just do a simple Google search of the company plus the word "reviews." Take all online reviews with a grain of salt, because there are always two sides to a story.

Sadly, not every reviewer acts in good faith and will withhold vital details to support their own perspective. I published a series of videos about reviews found on Trustpilot. The issue with that website is it's a magnet for disgruntled customers. Since self-publishing services or companies rarely encourage satisfied customers to report their experiences, you'll find that companies like KDP and Draft2Digital have low ratings, while companies like BookBaby and Blurb receive higher ratings.

You can also investigate most US-based companies through the Better Business Bureau (BBB) which has a database of insights and reviews. Most companies will work with the BBB to keep a good rating for fear of getting a dreaded low score. But sites like Trustpilot? Yeah, some companies put as much weight on Trustpilot as they do Yelp.

Ask around. Get feedback from other authors and collect as much as you can from many sources, so you have a balanced view of every website or platform. Not everyone is going to love KDP or Draft2Digital, so it's your job to figure out why they feel that way so you can make an informed decision.

Conversely, get all the positive intel about the companies you're looking to explore so you can feel a bit more comfortable and validated in the direction you're headed.

Most important of all: Take your time! Do not rush your research and never leave a question unanswered before exploring a website or service. Unanswered questions can lead to future hassles!

## CHECK PRICING & ROYALTY TRANSPARENCY

Every self-publishing company comes with an asterisk for access to their services. Whether you're looking to use KDP for its revenue share model or PublishDrive for its monthly subscription rates, every website comes with a catch.

When I can't find an answer, I simply contact support for that platform. If I can't get a straightforward answer, either I decide not to choose that path or push forward knowing those limitations. For instance, when I reached out to Author's Republic for a full breakdown of royalties per partner, they stated it was confidential information. No one will truly know what the royalty is for a specific partner until they get paid, and even then, there are still questions, especially when you've enrolled in a subscription-based model.

In contrast, you can easily find the royalty agreement per partner when using Findaway Voices by Spotify for distribution. If you prefer not having that information withheld, Findaway Voices might be the better option for you.

Around mid-2023, I published a four-part video series where I compared various print-on-demand companies based on their base costs, shipping fees, and other various metrics (link in Resources). I specifically wanted to illustrate the difference between pricing and quality for each platform, but more importantly, I wanted authors to be more discerning about the print-on-demand company they choose.

Many new authors blindly follow other authors or YouTubers without fully sifting through the options for ebook, print book, and audiobook distribution. Believe it or not, Amazon isn't the only game in town. While they dominate most online publishing profits, they don't capture all the market share.

If you want publishing to pay you like a business, you must treat it as such. This means you need to vet and leverage companies that align with your business needs and goals. In the event you're pursuing wide publishing just for fun, I'll stand down. Just know that if you want to get yourself back on track later, it might require a little extra work you should've done from the start.

## ASSESS DISTRIBUTION OPTIONS

Publishing wide is all about reaching more readers while also getting paid for your hard work. But there comes a point when you have to evaluate what's moving the needle in your business. Anyone aiming to reach as many platforms as possible should explore every available option. The more discerning author needs to explore each avenue to see if it's worth the extra time to publish there, then proceed according to the best use of their time.

This means as you go through each of the previous checklists, decide if one avenue is even worth pursuing. When in doubt, try it out for one book. Measure the results after a year, then see if it makes more sense to focus your attention on a narrower approach to publishing.

For all authors, I strongly suggest using email marketing. Start gathering your engaged readers through an email list. This safeguards you from being deplatformed and losing your audience. If you're terminated from KDP or any other platform, you'll at least have some of your readers on speed dial. Then you can share what happened and where else readers can find your books.

I always recommend having a direct sales option ready, because the more self-sufficient you can become, the better. The only exception to using direct sales is if your ebook is exclusive to the KDP Select program or your audiobook is exclusive in ACX. You do not have to publish all your books wide, so don't be afraid to keep your ebook exclusive on KDP Select if you like it. Or, if you prefer keeping your audiobook exclusively on ACX, leave it there.

Currently, no print-on-demand platform requires exclusivity, so you have every capability to set up a direct sales page on your website or through services like Payhip.

For ebooks or audiobooks not opted into exclusivity contracts, sell them direct. You have little to lose since places like Laterpress, Payhip, or Gumroad will gladly host your files for no cost while taking a fraction of sales.

## READ THE FINE PRINT

Your copyright is priceless—protect it carefully. In early 2024, Findaway Voices by Spotify faced backlash after updating their Terms of Use, which many interpreted as a blatant rights grab. Account holders quickly raised concerns, prompting a swift public outcry. Within two days, Spotify revised the Terms of Use to improve the wording to make it less exploitative and more transparent.

Always read the fine print.

I understand that most platform agreements are dry, boring, and chock full of legalese, but it's your responsibility to know what's at stake. I can't tell you how many authors I've heard violated the rules for various platforms, often through minor mistakes.

For instance, quite a few KDP account holders find out the hard way that you should not open multiple accounts. Amazon terminates duplicate or alternate accounts they believe to be held by one person. I reached out to the KDP Team to clarify this point a bit more since some folks believe if you can open multiple accounts with unique business IDs. To paraphrase their answer, "One account per person. No exceptions."

You'll find some other rather arbitrary rules, so be prepared to ask questions or bear the risk of violating an agreement. And don't merely choose to ignore a rule based on what others experience. I had a friend who published nude photography books with some images bordering on pornography (because of the implied sexual acts). Well, he got suspended and was told to correct his issues. He did, but within a few weeks, KDP terminated his account due to multiple infractions found in his backlog.

That friend tried pushing back by sharing all the examples of books published that definitely violate the Terms & Conditions. KDP didn't care about that proof. They upheld their decision, and the others got off scot-free.

The adage goes:

> *Just because everyone else jumps off a bridge doesn't mean you have to.*

When you need answers, you can always consult an attorney or contact customer support. Don't rely on advice from random people online or artificial intelligence. Your author business depends on you knowing and following the rules.

## TEST CUSTOMER SUPPORT SERVICES

Yep, it seems rather silly, but quite a few authors don't look for answers from the source. Countless viewers leave comments on my channel asking about what they should do on a specific platform. Though I appreciate the engagement, authors need to contact platform support, even if it's not that great.

That's why the first thing you should do with any platform before investing any time publishing through them is to test the support features. I've found that KDP Support (available through the Contact Us link in the bottom of your dashboard) can be helpful as long as you're picking the right option. Phone support and live chat support have proven immensely helpful in my many times using them. Email support? It's very much lacking and I recommend most authors avoid it if they have more pressing issues beyond asking for price matching and general platform advice.

You'll need to find that out for yourself, so your first major step after setting up an account should be to contact support. Come with a laundry list of questions that you couldn't otherwise get answered through a quick browse in the Terms & Conditions or a Google search. Support services will show you what they're made of real fast based on the response you get and when you get it.

I've found all the platforms I've suggested have great customer support options, but I don't want that to influence how *you* feel about their services. You must take a platform for a test drive to truly know if it's a good fit for you.

## ORDERING PROOFS FOR ALL ITERATIONS

In order to truly understand the reader experience, you must go through the process like a reader does. This doesn't mean you have to read your book for the fifty-millionth time, but you should buy a proof of your book in every iteration available. This includes ebooks, print books, and audiobooks.

I have a copy of all of my books for many reasons:

1. To see how the reading experience holds up once it's live through a website.
2. To double-check for any errors missed in the publishing process.
3. To share with other people, both in person and online.

I understand some authors work on a limited budget, so if you're hard-pressed to afford proofs, you can always drop the price as low as you can or order wholesale copies (also known as author copies).

When I launch a book, I buy the ebook, both print book iterations, and the audiobook. The first thing I do is open the book and do a quick flip through all the contents. This means downloading and opening my ebook in a Kindle reader app or Kindle device. Print books require a little more hands-on scrutiny. Look for how the pages appear, if there are any wonky formatting issues, and also, are there any misprints. Believe it or not, print-on-demand companies are far from perfect. Avoid using companies that consistently produce print books below your expectations. For audiobooks, I'll listen to the content in 2x, so I don't have to invest more time than I already have in production.

Ordering proofs isn't about frivolous spending, but about auditing quality and assuring the reader is getting the absolute best from you and the company you're using.

## ADDITIONAL OPTIONS & ALTERNATIVES

The beauty of self-publishing is that it's like a choose-your-own-adventure book. You've got so many more options to explore beyond what I've offered in this book. For instance, you can repurpose your content in several ways:

1. **Translations**: Tap into foreign translation rights for your publication. You can translate your book into many languages and distribute even more from one manuscript. Any author feeling overwhelmed or unsure if translating books is a good fit should consider selling their foreign translation rights through platforms like PubMatch.
2. **Miscellaneous options**: People are still listening to audiobooks on CD or cassette. It's a niche market, but one

worth pursuing if your audience is clamoring for this option. Sadly, I don't know of many print-on-demand companies that produce CDs and cassettes, so do your research. Be prepared to invest a little up front to get these treasured relics.

3. **Videos**: You can turn audiobooks into videos to distribute through platforms like YouTube or placed behind a paywall through platforms like Payhip or Gumroad. Nonfiction authors can easily turn their manuscript into a video script, providing a ready-made course to sell to their audience. Not all folks will read or listen to a book, but some are eager to check it out in video form. I've done this with great success!

4. **Low-content books**: These types of books are typically diaries, journals, notebooks, workbooks, planners, and more. They require minor work compared to writing and producing literature but act as a great companion for your flagship products. For instance, I had a book called *The 90-Day Home Workout Plan*, so I created a *90-Day Home Workout Journal* with all the workouts featured in the book. At a loss for ideas on how low content books work for your author business? Ask your readers; they'll give clear answers about what they crave most.

## MY FINAL THOUGHTS ON RESEARCH

Wouldn't it be nice to open up a book or pick up a course that provides the most comprehensive coverage on self-publishing? The reality is no one can truly cover all aspects of the business without missing a few elements or tainting the information with personal

## STEP 3: HIT THE CHECKLIST

Access all dashboards to the companies where you have accounts. You know the neat little trick I shared earlier, so open all windows from the bookmarks folder for audiobook publishing companies. Now it's time to get to work.

# THE WIDE PUBLISHING CHECKLIST FOR AUDIOBOOKS

- [ ] Audiobook Creation Exchange (ACX): Since you're publishing wide, you must choose non-exclusive. Ignore the option for Apple; Findaway Voices will be the de facto distributor since they're a preferred Apple partner.

- [ ] Kobo Writing Life: Once you request and get access, your audiobook can publish to Kobo, Kobo Plus, and OverDrive.

- [ ] Google Play Books Partner Center: You can upload your own audio files or use the GPBPC dashboard to generate digital narration. While the quality isn't perfect, it's a budget-friendly choice for those with limited resources.

- [ ] Findaway Voices by Spotify
  - [ ] Deselect any of the previously used options:
    - [ ] Amazon/Audible
    - [ ] Google Play Books
    - [ ] Kobo, Kobo Plus, and Overdrive

- [ ] Author's Republic
  - [ ] If you plan to use both Findaway Voices and Author's Republic, remove these overlapping avenues in one of your accounts: 24Symbols,

biases. That's why you should do the research and determine the best path forward based on your goals and needs.

I understand it's a pain and some folks would rather relegate research to other folks. Platforms like BookBaby exist because some authors don't want to bother exploring multiple options. They'd rather pay money to *not* have to worry about it.

Sadly, that's where vanity publishing companies thrive. To the uninitiated, throwing money at the problem seems like the best solution, but it doesn't always return the same results.

There's no other way to say this than as simply as possible:

*Do your research.*

# CONCLUSION

Some dusty bin in my storage closet has a copy of that old *Circus* magazine with my band in it. This brings me back to a time before the internet dominated our mental space. The magazine is a reminder of the days when I had hair on my head, a song in my heart, and an unending supply of hopeless enthusiasm. Did my band ever make it big? No. In fact, I believe our success peaked shortly after, in the early 2000s. We disbanded after finding other passions in our respective lives.

Thinking back, I often reflect on how our lives would've been so different if we had never submitted our band to *Circus* magazine. With limited reach, we would have had to rely on grinding it out. I'm sure we would have given up years sooner since we didn't feel like we had any true fans in the world. Getting that reach and exposure was monumental and was not something we took lightly.

The same goes for authors who choose to publish beyond the same old popular means of Kindle Direct Publishing and Audiobook Creation Exchange. While many authors successfully publish on Amazon's distribution avenues, others are hungry for more opportunities. Why not? You worked hard to produce a high-quality book. Why not get it in front of more readers? Should you find wide publishing doesn't provide the results you want, you can always delist your books on the respective platforms and go back to the comforts of Amazon exclusivity through the KDP Select program and ACX.

I'll think no differently of you should you choose to avoid publishing wide. Before you dismiss wide publishing, I want you to think about the one reader who doesn't use Amazon to buy books. How much of an impact could you make on their life if only you made your content more accessible? What would your career look like as an author if you veered off the path of least resistance? Could you make more money? Possibly, but could you reach more readers? Absolutely!

The only thing stopping you from publishing wide now is time. Don't let time slip by without sailing into uncharted waters. It's better to regret something you did than something you didn't do. Rather than wondering if publishing wide is for you, why don't you simply pull the trigger and *know* if it's a good fit?

Until that day, happy publishing!

## BEFORE YOU GO...

Your opinion matters! Whether you loved the book, found it helpful, or have suggestions, leaving a review wherever you purchased or downloaded it makes a huge difference. Reviews help other readers discover great books and give me valuable feedback to continue improving my work. I read every review and truly appreciate your time and input.

If you're hungry for more self-publishing insights, check out my other books at DaleLinks.com/Bookshelf. Also, feel free to connect with me directly or ask questions by joining my Discord community at DaleLinks.com/Discord.

Thank you for being part of my author journey!

# ABOUT THE AUTHOR

Dale L. Roberts is a self-publishing advocate, award-winning author, and trusted voice in the indie publishing community. With over fifty titles and forty-two literary awards to his name, Dale has established himself as a cornerstone of self-publishing success. His book, *Self-Publishing for New Authors*, is an entrant for the 2025 Pulitzer Prize for General Nonfiction.

As the founder of two YouTube channels—Dale L. Roberts, with over 100,000 subscribers, and the Self-Publishing with Dale Podcast, with over 14,000 subscribers—Dale reaches hundreds of thousands of aspiring and seasoned authors worldwide. His videos, lauded for their honesty, relatability, and to-the-point delivery, have garnered over 6.8 million views and nearly 500,000 hours of watch time.

Dale's deep connections with industry leaders, including Amazon KDP, Draft2Digital, and Findaway Voices, make him a valuable resource for authors navigating the ever-evolving publishing landscape. As a Video Content Advisor for the Alliance of Independent Authors, he's recognized for his innovative approach to content creation and author branding.

Beyond his professional success, Dale's journey is rooted in perseverance and passion. From self-publishing his first book on health and wellness in 2014 to overcoming early struggles through mentorship, Dale's story inspires authors to achieve their dreams. A former personal trainer and professional wrestler, Dale now dedicates his time to writing, creating music, and sharing life with his wife and their two rare, all-white rescue cats, Auggie and Allie.

> *"Being an indie author is so much more than writing and publishing books. It's about making real human connections and an impact that'll echo for generations to come." – Dale L. Roberts*

Relevant links:

- Website - SelfPublishingWithDale.com
- YouTube – Youtube.com/SelfPublishingWithDale
- My Books – DaleLinks.com/Bookshelf
- Discord – DaleLinks.com/Discord
- Facebook - Facebook.com/SelfPubWithDale
- X – X.com/SelfPubWithDale
- TikTok – TikTok.com/@selfpubwithdale
- Instagram – Instagram.com/SelfPubWithDale

## SPECIAL THANKS

I can't thank everyone that I'd like to, but I know there are a few superstars who've directly impacted my self-publishing career, both in books and videos. Mark Leslie Lefebvre and M.K. Williams are two great friends who published books about publishing wide, so their books were instrumental in the production of this book. I highly recommend checking out *Wide for the Win* by Mark Leslie Lefebvre and *Going Wide* by M.K. Williams (see Resources for links).

Big special thanks to the founder of Smashwords, Mark Coker, for his tireless efforts in building one of the best companies in aggregate self-publishing. Smashwords was the first platform I used beyond Amazon KDP and has treated me well ever since. Mark's a legend, especially considering all the headaches, hassle, and horse manure he had to endure being one of the first ebook sales platforms for indie authors. People labeled him a scammer and a charlatan for offering a platform to sell ebooks when no other place was doing it. When you get the chance, tune into the Smart Author Podcast; he shares more about his humble beginnings that'll make you appreciate what he did to pave the road we're walking on.

And I'm grateful to all the folks who've helped me from the various self-publishing companies including Kevin Tumlinson, Jim Azevedo,

Dan Wood, Kris Austin, Nick Thacker, Adam Woods, Danica Favorite, Kinga Jentetics, Julie Trelstad, Alex Smith, Luca Melero, Ray Johnson, Ann Zangri, Chelsea Bennett, and the KDP Team.

Of course, I can't mention my band without giving a shout-out and some love to my bandmates from Degenerate Godz, Mahoney, and Paraviolence: First and foremost, my other brother, Tobey Riddle, because he's been my ride-or-die for years. The dude will literally give you the shirt off his back and will stop at nothing to make you feel loved and appreciated. Also, Walter Roberts, Harold Webb, Donnie Dunn (RIP), Russ Webster, Tom Corbin, Mark Maxwell, Casey Kelvington, Chris Stone, and Joe Stout.

Another special heartfelt thank you to my beta readers, Ava Fails and William D. Latoria. I appreciate them taking the time to read, scrutinize, and provide notes for this book. If you're a reader and want to check out a couple of great indie authors, pick up one of their books.

Last, my deepest and most heartfelt gratitude goes to someone who has profoundly impacted both my life and my career: Jeanne De Vita. Your unwavering support, unmatched talent, and genuine kindness have made all the difference. I'm forever grateful for the countless ways you've lifted me up, guided me, and believed in me. You are, without question, one of the brightest lights in my world, and I am endlessly thankful for you. Thank you for everything—you are truly one of a kind.

# RESOURCES

- Draft2Digital – DaleLinks.com/D2D
- *Kobo Writing Life Live Q&A* – DaleLinks.com/KWLLive
- The Alliance of Independent Authors (ALLi) – DaleLinks.com/ALLi
- International ISBN Agency – DaleLinks.com/ISBN
- PublishDrive's Calculator – Calculator.PublishDrive.com
- Lulu's Pricing Calculator – Lulu.com/Pricing
- Metadata Sheet – DaleLinks.com/MetadataSheet
- Calibre – Calibre-ebook.com
- Amazon's Send to Kindle – Amazon.com/SendToKindle
- Kindlepreneur's Free Barcode Generator – DaleLinks.com/Barcode
- Bookvault's Guide to Payhip – DaleLinks.com/BookvaultPayhip
- Audiobook Creation Exchange's Guidelines – DaleLinks.com/ACXGuidelines
- Writer Beware – WriterBeware.blog
- Trustpilot Reviews for Amazon KDP & Other Self-Publishing Companies – DaleLinks.com/Trustpilot
- *Going Wide* by MK Williams – DaleLinks.com/GoingWide
- *Wide for the Win* by Mark Leslie Lefebvre – DaleLinks.com/WideForTheWin

# REFERENCES

i	GeoRiot Network, Inc. (2023 March 15). 10 Fascinating Audiobook Statistics. https://booklinker.com/blog/audiobook-stats/

ii	Apple Inc. (No date). Book Availability. https://itunespartner.apple.com/books/articles/book-availability-2741

iii	Apple Inc. (No date). Digital narration technology. https://authors.apple.com/support/4519-digital-narration-audiobooks

iv	Apple Inc. (No date). Apple Books Payments. https://itunespartner.apple.com/books/articles/apple-books-payments-2748

v	Rakuten Kobo Inc. (No date.) Where else can Kobo distribute my eBooks? https://kobowritinglife.zendesk.com/hc/en-us/articles/360059385751-Where-else-can-Kobo-distribute-my-eBooks-

vi	Friedman, Jane. (2019 July 2). Public Libraries: How Authors Can Increase Both Discoverability and Earnings. https://www.janefriedman.com/public-libraries-how-authors-can-increase-both-discoverability-and-earnings/.

vii	Rakuten Kobo Inc. (2021 February 18.) Reach More Readers with OverDrive. https://kobowritinglife.com/2021/02/18/reach-more-readers-with-overdrive/

# REFERENCES

viii     Rakuten Kobo Inc. (2021 November 4.) 5 Reasons to Enroll Your Books in Kobo Plus. https://kobowritinglife.com/2021/11/04/5-reasons-to-enroll-your-books-in-kobo-plus/

ix     Rakuten Kobo Inc. (2021 August.) What will my earnings be?. https://kobowritinglife.zendesk.com/hc/en-us/articles/360058976032-What-will-my-earnings-be-

x     Google. (No date.) Supported countries for selling books on Google Play. https://support.google.com/books/partner/table/6052428?hl=en

xi     Google. (no date). Revenue Split FAQs https://support.google.com/books/partner/answer/9331459

xii     Draft2Digital. (no date). Knowledge Base. https://www.draft2digital.com/knowledge-base/

xiii     Mandi Lynn. (2023 June 18). Why I Will Never Work With IngramSpark Again. https://youtu.be/RDRryxTX30M?si=VQgF0qiDtMMtTgjn

xiv     Lulu Press, Inc. (2024 September 20). Creator Revenue: The Basics. https://help.lulu.com/en/support/solutions/articles/64000255464-creator-revenue-the-basics

xv     Audible, Inc. (no date). Narrate an audiobook. https://help.acx.com/s/article/producing-and-recording-your-audiobook

www.ingramcontent.com/pod-product-compliance
Lightning Source LLC
Chambersburg PA
CBHW071714020426
42333CB00017B/2261